Spirit Lake People

Memories of Mount St. Helens

D1453296

Spirit Lake People

Memories of Mount St. Helens

by
Alan Guggenheim

Edited by James Mortland

SALEM PRESS
GRESHAM, OREGON
1986

First Edition 1986

Salem Press
Post Office Box 3158
Gresham, Oregon 97030

Edited by James Mortland
Text set in Goudy Old Style by Paul O. Giesey/Adcrafters
Printed and bound by BookCrafters
Library of Congress Cataloging-in-Publication Data
Guggenheim, Alan, 1950-
    Spirit Lake people.
1. Saint Helens, Mount, Region (Wash.) — Biography.
2. Saint Helens, Mount, Region (Wash.) — Social life and customs. I. Mortland, James.
II. Title.
F897.S17G84   1986   979.7'84   86-62235

ISBN 0-910377-08-1 (soft)

To my parents

Gustave Nathan Guggenheim
Ina Elouise Hays Guggenheim

ACKNOWLEDGMENTS

Spirit Lake People began as a personal research project six years ago. Locating sources was slow and arduous until Paul Pintarich, book review editor for *The Oregonian*, gave my work some notice in his column in the June 9, 1985 issue of *Northwest Magazine*.

Two days later, Rick Harmon, oral historian for the Oregon Historical Society, offered me access to a cardboard box of two dozen uncatalogued oral histories of people who lived, worked and played around Spirit Lake the past 85 years. The composite "memories" of Mount St. Helens that I have constructed in *Spirit Lake People* would not have been possible without the gracious and scholarly assistance of Mr. Harmon and the library staff of the Oregon Historical Society. I wish to extend special thanks to Thomas Vaughan, director of the Oregon Historical Society and himself a longtime habitue of Spirit Lake.

I am indebted to William Lange, son of pioneer Robert Charles Lange, and his family for helping me convey the essence of turn-of-the-century life in the peculiar wilderness of Spirit Lake.

Francis Lambert, a lifelong Portland resident, former Multnomah County sheriff and a holder of numerous civic and charitable organization posts, died in 1985, a year too soon see the publication of his Spirit Lake memory back in 1913. He attributed his long list of accomplishments to the solid foundation laid during his youth by adults such as John C. Meehan, the first man to open a youth camp on Spirit Lake.

Amos Lawrence, a longtime Portland artist and educator now living back East, took a special interest in *Spirit Lake People* and was vital in my detective work regarding the origin of the hairy apes story that ran on the front pages of *The Oregonian* during the week of July 13, 1924.

Very little remains of the exploits of Northwest mountaineer Lige Coalman, and I had about given up finding anything meaningful on his life until the Multnomah County Library reference desk uncovered Victor H. White's *The Story of Lige Coalman*, published by St. Paul's Press, Sandy, Oregon, in 1972. I thank Don Weber, manager of St. Paul's Press, for granting me permission to quote passages from the book and also for keeping this intriguing little volume in print and available to the public.

Harmony Falls Lodge came alive to me during some pleasant conversations with Julia Schauffler Bernard, and John W.S. and Jane Kerr Platt. Their memories enrich us all. I regret having never attended one of Aunt Deedlie's parties.

Jake Jones was 28 in 1938. Today, he is pushing 80 but still as feisty and hard as a gunnysack full of ball bearings. After long hours of interviews, Mr. Jones shrewdly advised me to "get out of the office and get into the woods or you'll die an early death." He is proof of what a life spent outdoors around Spirit Lake — or any other wilderness setting — can do for a man. Thanks for the advice, Jake.

The U.S. Forest Service provided some great people to maintain order in the Spirit Lake region of the Gifford Pinchot National Forest since the turn of the century: Harold "Sam" Samuelson, Jim Langdon, Helen Leonard, Hazel Marcellus, Fred Bradley, Bob Lambert, Rant Mullins, Bill Allen and many, many more. I hope my deep respect and appreciation for the Forest Service — with its mission impossible of pleasing everybody — comes through loud and clear.

Somewhere out there is a woman named Patty Otis Dyke. I was not able to track her down, but her written recollection of Camp Westwind on Spirit Lake, which she left with the Oregon Historical Society, proved invaluable. I wish to thank her for sharing that memory.

I also thank the Longview Ski Club's many charter members, including the Cripes and the Quoidbachs, the Wests and Gunnar Nilsson. Mr. Nilsson is an expert source on both the plant life of St. Helens and the Saturday night wildlife at the ski club lodge. He was a friend to Harry Truman and Jack Nelson, Ole Peterson and Jake Jones. An accomplished botanist, printmaker and photographer, Mr. Nilsson's work deserves greater public appreciation.

Noel McRae and Susan Saul merit special thanks. Ms. Saul certainly deserved Gulf Oil's Citizen Conservation Award in 1983 for her efforts in the bureaucratic trenches, fighting for creation of the Mount St. Helens National Volcanic Monument. Mr. McRae is a dreamer who does not give up easily.

I thank Silas Scoggins, former "ghostbuster" of Spirit Lake Lodge, whose monthly phone calls to see how the book was coming kept my own spirits from flagging. Do you really think I could land a big salmon at Cascade Locks, Silas?

Finally, thank you Cheryl, Adam and Jeffrey for accompanying dad on those many weekend trips to Mount St. Helens. Your interest and curiosity in Mount St. Helens fueled me with the energy to finish *Spirit Lake People*. My sons should make fine volcanologists for the U.S. Geological Survey.

Gresham, Oregon, 1986

Contents

Spirit Lake People

Chapter I

Seeahtiks—Lost Souls of Spirit Lake

Like wisps of smoke out of the lodge smokehole, much of the Indian legends and lore about Lawelatla, or "Smoking Mountain," has been lost. Fortunately though, some fragments of stories have filtered down to us, and from them we can gain a picture of how the Indians viewed this mountain we call St. Helens. Let us imagine ourselves gathered around the campfire in one of the tribal lodges 200 years ago.

Winter in the Cowlitz country. Time for stories. Icy night winds course down the lower reaches of the white-capped Columbia River. Bluish smoke threads its way out the tops of a dozen Indian lodges encrusted with freezing rain and blowing snow. A pack of half-wild dogs scurries for shelter under a row of canoes banked upside down on drying racks. Slippery fishing platforms stand naked and abandoned in the icy green river.

Inside the lodge, a dozen Indian children burrow into layers of bear hides and buckskins. There is little to do but gnaw on dried jerky, sip herb tea and wait for Grandfather, the teller of stories.

An old woman flips a chunk of split alder the size of her arm on the fire and then rushes out the flap door of the lodge. Ashes fly. The air fills with smoke and crackling sounds. The children rub their eyes. Grandfather enters the lodge with a faint whooshing sound and plops down on a thick bed of skins behind the fire, his face fully lit. A silence descends on the group.

"Hah-yeh-do, yeh-do-waaah!" he chants over and over. Quietly at first, he sings, his gravelly voice gradually rising in tempo until his feet are tapping the ground and his hands, palms outstretched, are rising and falling. The fire pops. Smoke swirls around his leathery face, hideous with a crazyquilt of scars from the claws of a crazed black bear many years before. The children lean forward, entranced by his stern visage, as if peering into a cave at some ominous presence, fierce and curious, a shadow of some supernatural being. There is silence once again.

"What do you give me if I tell you stories?" asks the old one.

"Bowls of sweetmeats and smoked fish?" offers one of the boys.

"Naw! I should leave," Grandfather scowls.

"Kinnikinnick to smoke and huckleberries to eat?" offers an older boy hidden in the shadows.

"Hah!" the old one spits into the fire. "Very good! And where do you get the huckleberries?" he fires back.

"From Loo-wit, home of evil spirits," the young buck answers.

"Ooooh-whooo, the Seeahtiks! You take great risks picking huckleberries beneath the snowy mountain we call Loo-wit. For that is the summer domain of the Seeahtiks. Big-breasted giants, shaggy monsters strong enough to pull the heads off People."

The children snuggle closer to one another. Grandfather continues:

"The lake at the foot of beautiful Loo-wit is home to Seeahtiks. Neither man nor animal, the Seeahtik can imitate the bird or make the splashing sound of the waterfall."

The old man blinks, looks upward, then makes the sound of water cascading off rocks and wind ripping the air: "Kuuuhssssh." He finishes the sound effect, glancing at the young people huddled all around him, motionless, breathless.

"They winter far to the north and fish in the rivers around Loo-wit. But in mid-summer the Seeahtik make their homes on the banks of Spirit Lake. You can hear their strange noises echoing in the valleys, so stay away, stay away!"

He pauses, raising two fingers to his mouth, and then blows them away.

"Only the strongest and shrewdest braves can survive a trip to Spirit Lake. But go we all must if we are to find our Tamanaweis, our soul power. You too will go. Someday. Just beware, the Seeahtiks!"

He pauses again. His chest heaves as if summoning his own courage, and

2

then he continues:

"They cry like a wolf. They can trick you. Kill one of them and they will kill twelve of you. Tall, narrow-hipped, crooked legs, deep chests, their black eyes glitter like those of the bird. Their jaws are massive. They are strange, I tell you, they lack souls. They were animals. They would be men. But the Great Spirit decided they were evil and refused to fill them with Tamanaweis, soul power."

The boys up front gasp. The old one waits for silence.

"When I was a young brave many, many years ago, I came upon eight of the Seeahtik. I had walked all day down an underground trail and was lost. They looked up at me and bid me a strange welcome to their camp. I sat with them around their campfire. They ate a beast which they had hypnotized before killing with their bare hands. They tore the flesh from the bones and stuffed their mouths with wads as big as your head. They wiped their greasy paws on their naked sides and talked among themselves in a queer, animal language I could not understand.

"The Seeahtik drink from Spirit Lake. Beware of that lake. In it lives a demon so huge its hand can stretch clear across the northern reach and drag a fisherman's canoe into the depths of that bottomless lake.

"And fish! Beware the fish with the head of a bear and the teeth of a mountain lion. They cast a spell over Spirit Lake that lures the young brave in search of his manhood. Ghosts of deer and elk dart just out of the range of the young warrior's bow. The urge to track these animals is irresistable and leads the brave to the shore of Spirit Lake. There, the demons stretch out their long arms and pull the hapless warrior under."

The tallest brave in the lodge sits up on his knees and throws out a challenge to the old one. "I am strong, I know my soul has the power to defy Spirit Lake. I know, I know . . ."

"You are foolish. Sit down," the old one barks, suddenly enraged at the young brave's defiance, not of him the storyteller, rather of the forces of nature that could take his life in a moment. The old one thinks a while, deciding on a fitting response to the cocksure brave.

"There once was a man, a proud uncle. His nephew was a courageous, young brave, a young and powerful man, like you. The brave tracked a big-horned goat up a river to the outlet of Spirit Lake. The demon reached out and grabbed the brave for the goat was only a ghost, bait to trick the young warrior. The brave uncle fought long and fought hard, to pull the boy from the jaws of the ferocious demon but it bit the young brave neatly in two."

Wind howls outside the lodge as the storm's intensity nears its peak. Grandfather stares back into the wide-open eyes of his charges.

3

"Listen now, for the Seeahtik may be outside this very lodge.

"Listen! Three whistles signal their advance. The pelting of the walls by stones the size of your finger indicates they are close.

"Listen! They speak in the tongues of all animals.

"Listen! They speak in the tongue of the wind.

"Listen! They can make themselves invisible by rubbing strange medicine on their hairy bodies.

"When you smell their rank odor of rot and death it is too late. Prepare to wake from your sleep, lost and alone on the snowy heights of Loo-wit. For that is where you will be if the giants steal you away under their skin before you wake."

Suddenly, from the middle of the huddle of children comes the plaintive cry, "Grandfather!" The old one recognizes the voice of his favorite grandson, eleven years old and straightbacked, a hunter already, destined someday to lead the small band.

"Grandfather! Is there no hope for us from the Seeahtik?"

Grandfather spits hard into the fire. The reflections of the flames dance mischievously in the old one's eyes. His gnarled hands rise, palms up, so that the youth of his tribe can glimpse the trail of wrinkles etched in his leathery skin.

"These hands, my sad-eyed grandson, held the Seeahtik by the throat and shook him 'til he let loose of my soul." Grandfather cracks a toothless smile. "Hah-hah-hah-hah! Ptoooi! on Seeahtik if your soul is strong, my young friend."

"How do I strengthen my soul, Grandfather?"

"Laugh, dream, harden your will power, resist silliness, embrace your People and remember Our ways. Do this and you will be strong enough against the Seeahtik, the unknown and whatever else the Evil Spirit hurls on you. Mountains may move but you must not flinch. Your will to survive must withstand the tides, the winds, even the shaking of the Universe. Then, Seeahtik can't touch you."

Chapter II

Grandpa Lange — The Man Who Opened Spirit Lake

Pioneer Robert Charles Lange cut the road to Spirit Lake through virgin forests back during the turn of the century, but he never lived to see it paved.

At the age of 81, he folded up one Saturday a week and a half before Christmas from the pain of a heart attack. Death dropped the Spirit Lake pioneer and self-made man in his tracks, muddy that morning from the cold December rain. His body embraced the road he built in front of the mountain home he built beneath the cold, impassive stare of Mount St. Helens. The year was 1933.

Back in their cabin was Lange's wife Minnie Foron Lange. A true child of the Northwest, her parents, both of French ancestry, had traveled west by covered wagon. Minnie grew up on tales of the prairie crossing, especially those of encounters with Indians and the elements. She knew in her heart the bravery expected of her that cold day in December when she lost her husband. But how would she get the body down the mountain for the funeral arrangements?

Minnie Foron married Robert Charles Lange in 1887, shortly after he returned from his first prospecting trip to Spirit Lake. He was searching for gold, but had discovered instead a lush wooded region surrounding an incredibly deep, blue lake, frosty and cold, a shimmering gem at the foot of snowy, symmetrical Mount St. Helens. He filled Minnie with tales of the richly forested realm beneath an incredible, round-shouldered snow cone. She took to this hard-working dreamer and his dream and asked to see St. Helens for herself.

"Someday," he replied. "Someday."

There was no road into Spirit Lake back then. To spend a few days prospecting around the mountain, Lange had to hike into the backcountry with a fully loaded pack. He cached his supplies near the lake outlet at the Toutle River. Then he hiked back out again for a second load. The trip from Castle Rock to his cache took three days.

The hikes strengthened his legs. He learned the hilltops and discovered the sweet smack of berries from the huckleberry bush. He saw some awfully big bears.

An immigrant born in Lodz, Poland, Lange was wise to the world. He had come to America at the age of 20, living successively in New York, Nebraska and Missouri before moving to the Northwest. The young man lived a while in Portland, then moved to Toledo. It was there he met and courted Miss Minnie Foron, later marrying her in Puyallup, Washington.

In 1892, three years after Washington became a state, pressure from miners including Lange prompted the creation of the St. Helens Mining District. Periodic spells of "gold fever" brought farmers from the settlements below, but few miners persisted with the tenacity of Lange.

Five years later, in 1897, Mount St. Helens was included in the creation of a federal forest reserve, destined to become part of the Columbia National Forest in 1908. By the time the U.S. Forest Service built a guard station at Spirit Lake in 1910, Lange had already mined a hundred-thousand tons of ore, sawn thousands of board feet of timber, drawn up plans for a store, applied for a permit to operate a post office and done a little farming in the "unfarmable" soil beneath Mount St. Helens. He grew hearty oats for the horses and plump strawberries, red and ripe, for the kids.

Throughout the first 20 summers on St. Helens, Minnie Foron Lange supported her multitalented dreamer of a husband even though chances were slim that he would make it rich on ore in so remote a location. The long haul to smelting facilities in Tacoma ate up his chances for hefty profits. Minnie continued her support when he decided to seek out additional working capital in Germany and mechanize his mining efforts. It was Minnie, with her deft hand at huckleberry pie-making, who turned the cabin Lange built below Spirit Lake into a summer home.

Soon, children danced in the meadow near the cabin. With the births of Ted and Julia, William, Georgia and Lillian, the Lange homesteaders discovered real gold.

Lange refocused his mining efforts after raising a second round of venture capital in Europe. He also got on with the county road department and made it his dream to lay in a road to Spirit Lake where only a well-worn Indian path existed. Pressure on County Commissioner Studebaker, from Lange and other prospectors, resulted in 1901 with the construction supervised by Lange of the first wagon road from Castle Rock to Spirit Lake.

In the early 1900s, he purchased $75,000 worth of electric machinery, powered by an ingenious waterwheel generator. Toting the equipment up from the flatlands by horse-drawn sled was difficult enough. Once at the headwaters of the north side of Spirit Lake, Lange then transferred the machinery to heavy, flat-bottomed scows, squared at both ends. The boats sank to the tops of their gunwales for the nervous crossing of Spirit Lake to the mining site below the 5,858-foot Mount Margaret, north of Spirit Lake. Copper-rich ore would have to be brought out the same way. Tailings were dumped where 20 years later Harry Truman would make his famed Mount St. Helens Lodge at the Spirit Lake outlet to the Toutle River.

The mine near the northwest end of the lake included a cluster of buildings in which the electric lights always glowed. The elevation was close to 4,000 feet. The power generated by the overshot Pelton wheel from water gushing through the pipe laid down the mountainside was sufficient to drive the mining equipment, the light bulbs and the saw in a makeshift lumber mill. Since the power was free, there was never a need to turn off the lights. Later, after the mine petered out, the mill and the Pelton wheel would be moved to the southwest end of the lake nearer the homestead.

Lange bulled his way through the woods, constantly talking of the future. He rarely flinched from his duty to family or his devotion to work. He would not be distracted either, even when Mount St. Helens erupted with small-scale steam explosions in 1898, 1903 and 1921. Every year right up to his death, Lange maintained plans sufficient for keeping himself busy the next 20 years. In winters, Lange kept the books for his brother-in-law who operated a fuel yard in Chehalis. In the summers, he was back proving up his land claim at Spirit Lake.

A fire at Lange's mine in the summer of 1908, started by smudge pots intended to keep flies off the horses' backs, burned the forest on the southern exposure of Mount Margaret. Still, Lange persisted in his effort to mine gold, silver and copper. The richest of the metal veins was copper, but clearly the vein was about played out.

Lange's German investors sent a mining engineer to assist in exploration, but his gruffness and strange nature alienated the miners. He brought with him 20 pairs of shoes and used a style of "high" English that amused more than impressed his hosts. "Transport the potatoes," he would say, instead of "Pass the potatoes." In the end though, it was the engineer's errors in judgement that caused the miners to undercut the veins and prompted several of Lange's crew members to quit one summer.

There were other miners too, some of whom befriended the stocky Pole. The St. Helens Mining District, organized on September 22, 1892, had attracted large amounts of investment capital. Claims were staked north of the mountain to the Green River Valley. The biggest problem was transporting ore out of the mining district to refineries a hundred miles away. It would take a rich ore indeed to override the high shipping costs.

Dr. Henry Coe mined the claim next to Lange's and was a friend and frequent acquaintance to the Spirit Lake pioneer. Coe, previously with the Alaska Sanatorium for the Insane in Portland, meticulously organized and supervised work on his claim and even sold stock to Teddy Roosevelt. Copper ore mined from Coe's claim was used in the casting of the Sacajawea statue that stands today in Portland's Washington Park. Coe's claim gradually lost its color. Lange's too went plunk. By 1911, most outside investors lost interest and mining operations tapered off.

If mining had been Lange's reason for coming to Spirit Lake, lack of mining opportunity would not prompt him to leave. No. He had found something else in the region. Mining had become his excuse for his claim to the homestead.

From mining, Lange turned his attention to lumbering. In 1912, he took up a homestead and timber claim, partially abandoning the mining venture in favor of his newly constructed sawmill. Woodrow Wilson personally signed Lange's homestead claim in 1914, thus protecting his claim from the U.S. Forest Service's "protection."

Lange had originally welcomed the newly formed Forest Service in 1908 but grew concerned two years later with the rapid construction of guard stations on the shores of Spirit Lake. By 1913, the Forest Service had relocated its main ranger station in the town of Toutle to the guard station location on Spirit Lake. Plans were drawn up, too, for a series of fire lookouts, including one on the summit of St. Helens by 1917.

The sawmill was not a one-man affair. Lange put together crews for sorting and stacking. The water was captured 600 feet up a steep hill and started down through an eight-inch pipe. The diameter of the pipe narrowed at its base which terminated in a powerhouse that shook from the force of the water as it shot out 100 feet over a water wheel and down into the canyon below.

The sawmill was used in 1912 to supply lumber for construction of the new Portland YMCA camp that John C. Meehan was building on the south side of Spirit Lake. The Forest Service also bought lumber for its ranger station and the series of fire lookouts it planned on all the major peaks in the region, including the summit station. Lange cut 1,000 feet a day by himself. He hired a man to yip and winnie the horse down the hills drawing behind it the prized Douglas fir logs into the makeshift sawmill yard.

No crew was necessary for the actual milling operation. Lange preferred to cut the lumber his way, by himself. He sawed heavy, unplaned two-by-fours for the framing and two-by-sixes for the roofs. Cabins in this region had to be sturdy, constructed of vertical boards with battens on the outside. To withstand the heavy snowfall, roofs had to be steep. The task required the right materials and to that end Lange prided himself.

The sawmill was originally below Lange's mine on Mount Margaret but was moved to the outlet of Spirit Lake closer to his homestead cabin. Daughters Lillian, Julia Mae and Georgia bloomed in the high altitude while sons Ted and William hiked the trails and swam in the lake with the pale-faced city boys up from Portland for the YMCA camp program.

Summer life in Spirit Lake country at the 3,000-foot elevation was good for his family. They were stronger, healthier, than if they stayed in Chehalis year-round. Son William oftentimes baked cakes for the "Y" camp boys when they hiked into the region in 1915. William also would hike with the "Y" campers for three days at a time with J.C. Meehan leading the way into the trail-less wilderness. They had little more than a compass and Meehan's good sense to direct them.

Lillian had a special charge in her Spirit Lake summer life. Camera in hand, she would sit on the banks of Spirit Lake for hours on end, waiting for that moment early in the morning when the breeze died and St. Helens' reflection mirrored the real thing, with not a ripple.

As if the sawmill was not enough, Lange and his wife launched their own restaurant in the early 1920s. The main attraction was Mrs. Lange's huckleberry pie, the fruit for which was picked by the now-grown Lange children a gallon-bucket at a time from the bushy timberline of Mount St. Helens.

Increasingly, the Langes were outnumbered by other families retreating to the area. Recreational use of Spirit Lake was increasing. The handful of YMCA campers led on foot by J.C. Meehan in 1913 turned into a veritable legion of boys trucked in from Castle Rock in 1923. Spirit Lake Lodge, constructed in 1913, was replaced in 1928 by Holmstedt Lodge with room for

50 guests. New resorts and youth camps were coming, too.

Lange continued to work as hard as ever. He was amply rewarded. He looked 60, though he was fast approaching his 80s. Son William recalled that his father used to drink a quart of whiskey a day in the early 1920s even though the Eighteenth Amendment, enacted in 1919, made liquor illegal. He smoked too. It was not an uncommon sight to find Grandpa Lange, as he was known, puffing on a cigar, smoke swirling around his face, screwed up as usual in a fit of stern concentration.

Lange's doctor finally prevailed on him to slow down with his bad habits. He successfully warned Lange of the pitfalls ahead if he did not quit, especially the drinking. Thus he probably stretched out his active life a few more years. Lange's son, William, recalled the circumstances which led his father back to drinking:

One day in the early 1930s, Harry Truman, the newcomer up the way with big plans for a year-round tourist resort on Spirit Lake, offered Lange the specialty of Mount St. Helens Lodge: Moonshine. Again, Lange took to drink, recalled William.

William also remembered visiting from his new home in Portland and finding his father disoriented and unkempt. His hair was tousled and he swayed from the deleterious effects of the moonshine.

Finding his father back on the hard stuff bothered William. He and his sisters also became concerned about their parents living alone in the remote Spirit Lake district, but there was nothing to do that might dissuade the pioneer couple from spending their remaining years in the area that had brought them so much happiness. Even good lives come to an end, though.

* * *

Minnie Foron Lange spied the huddled mass that was her husband in the middle of the road in front of their cabin. Despite the pouring rain, she ran out to help him. He lay still. His arms were limp, his head heavy. She cradled his head and propped it up out of the water puddle. Then she tried lifting him by his armpits but quickly realized he was too heavy to drag to the house. She needed help. Running back to the cabin, she turned to her neighbors, refusing to believe he was dead.

Foremost among their good neighbors was U.S. Forest Service Ranger "Sam" Samuelson. She cranked her phone box desperately, but there was no immediate answer to her call. She rang again.

Lige Coalman and his son Elrod were working near enough to the ranger station by Spirit Lake to hear the phone ring the second time. Knowing Samuelson was on call, Coalman dashed through the unlocked door and answered the ringing. He was greeted by a woman's voice.

"My husband has fainted. He is in the rain and mud on the road in front of the house. I've managed to get his head up out of the water, but I can't move him," said Mrs. Lange. Coalman assured her help was on the way and hung up.

Elrod cranked the Model-T Ford and together with his father raced through an increasingly torrential downpour. The two miles took five minutes to travel, even in the rain on the deeply-rutted road. Coalman jumped from the running board before Elrod stopped the car and hopped around the deep puddles to Grandpa Lange's side. A big man weighing 250 pounds, Lange appeared very still for a fainting victim. Lige directed Elrod to help lift the pioneer and together they carried him 50 yards to the house.

Coalman applied artificial respiration. The minutes ticked away. No reaction. No heartbeat. Mrs. Lange cupped her hands to her mouth.

"It's no use, ma'am. He's gone," said Coalman. Grandpa Lange had been dead from the beginning.

The rain had not yet knocked out phone service down the mountain to Castle Rock. Coalman called Harry Gustafson, a son-in-law of the Langes, living with his wife Julia Mae in Chehalis.

"I'll take care of things. I know what to do. We'll be right there," Gustafson said. He and Coalman talked about the weather and what to expect. Gustafson then called the coroner at the Frank R. Hubbard Funeral Home in Kelso and together they started immediately for the Lange homestead.

Coalman comforted Mrs. Lange and discussed with Elrod the heavy run-off from the Forsyth Glacier that was flooding down the mountain.

"That creek gulch down the road is swollen by the storm. I'm sure the mud and water have flooded the road at Coal Creek," Coalman said. Elrod nodded. No car could negotiate that gullywasher. The road was a mess for another 20 miles beyond the rushy chasm. Nevertheless, Coalman sensed what was "right" from the look in Mrs. Lange's eyes. He sent Elrod back to the YMCA camp for help and 200 feet of heavy rope.

By stretching the rope across the gulch and tying it to trees on both sides, Coalman was able to rig a safety rope. The corpse was roped into a stretcher basket. Harry Truman and Ranger Samuelson helped carry the body down the mountain, stepping from boulder to boulder across the raging torrent. One hand on the death basket, the other on the safety rope, they waded across the flood. Silt and sand filled their boots, forcing them to stop occasionally to empty the contents.

The mountain road stretched on interminably. Upon reaching the undertaker's rig, Truman and the coroner loaded Lange's remains while Coalman, his son Elrod and Ranger Samuelson talked to Gustafson about the funeral arrangements.

"When we returned to Spirit Lake, tired, wet and weary, we had hiked many miles that day, half of it carrying the 250-pound weight of the dead man. We all felt it was a good service to a fine neighbor and friend," recalled Coalman many years later in Victor H. White's *The Story of Lige Coalman*.

There was a lot of big news in the newspapers at the time of Lange's death. Prohibition was repealed. A Nazi named Hitler was coming to power in Europe. The Depression was raging. And newly elected Franklin D. Roosevelt was announcing his revolutionary New Deal. Nevertheless, Lange's death made headlines in *The Oregonian* for the hearty pioneer was widely known as the trailblazer who opened the road to Spirit Lake.

Times had indeed changed from when he left his native Poland on September 15, 1853, at the age of 20, young and hopeful, strong and a dreamer. But when "Grandpa" Lange died at the age of 81, he was still young and hopeful, strong and a dreamer, a busy man at peace with himself and his surroundings there at Spirit Lake.

Chapter III

A New World For Francis

Francis was heading out the door of the YMCA when he overheard some of the older boys talking. He stopped in his tracks at the mention of the word: "Bigfoot!"

Francis crowded closer to the cluster of boys in the doorway of the YMCA building. It was a rainy, gray April day in Portland. The spell of Bigfoot raised the hackles on the back of 11-year-old Francis Lambert's neck.

"Mr. Meehan is going to take us to the "Y" camp right there at Spirit Lake again, right smack dab underneath Mount St. Helens," a boy of 14 said.

"You're kidding!" blurted out young Francis. "Where Bigfoot is?" He had heard many times the tales told by last year's campers, tales of Bigfoot prints and strange, unexplainable sightings of hairy, ape-like creatures. And now there would be a return trip!

"I'm a good camper. Can I go?" Francis asked.

"Naw. You're only 11. Ya' gotta be 12. Mr. Meehan doesn't want any cry babies," the boy said.

Francis dropped his chin. He fell back into the same gloomy mood he had been in since his horse, Petty, had died. To a young boy on the verge of becoming an adolescent in 1913, life had already dealt young Francis more

13

disappointment than he deserved. Maybe his dad could do something. Francis Lambert's dad could do anything!

Francis bolted from the circle of boys on the front steps of the "Y" building and sprinted down Fifth Avenue. He slowed a step at Burnside then shot across the busy thoroughfare just out of the way of the churning wheels of freight wagons pulled by snorting teams of horses. Horns honked. Heavily-laden lorries belched acrid blue smoke and hot exhaust. The boy breathed in the mixture of gassy fumes and animal odors as he ran north up Fourth Avenue into the throngs of Chinatown.

He worked his way down Flanders and then north again up Third Avenue to the corner of Glisan and the open doorway of The Independent Laundry: William T. Lambert, Proprietor.

Two different phones owned by competing companies ra-a-a-a-ng off the wall as young Francis flew through the door. His sister Winona smiled at Francis as she lifted the receiver to the Pacific Telephone Company's phone set. Francis only glanced at her, though. His attention was riveted on his father. Mr. Lambert caught Francis' piercing stare as he answered the other telephone, the one that belonged to Pacific's competitor, the Home Telephone Company.

"Hello! Independent Laundry. May I help you?" his father crooned into the phone. Francis lined up directly in front of his father, waiting his turn to speak. His father looked down at the boy, puzzled by the great expectations aglow in his clear blue eyes. Mr. Lambert could hardly pay attention to his call.

"Yes, yes, well okay, very well. We can take care of it," Mr. Lambert said. He hung up the phone, then to Francis said, "Well?"

The words spilled out of the boy.

"Dad there's a bunch o' guys at the "Y" talking about going camping at Spirit Lake, but you've got to be 12, ah, but I'm a good camper and . . ."

"Whoa, Francis. Slow down and start again," Mr. Lambert said.

The story sluiced out of Francis. Mr. Lambert nodded at his son's enthusiasm. But he sensed there was something more here. "Well, Francis, what do you know about Mount St. Helens? Why do you want to go so badly?"

"Bigfoot! The guys were talking and they said there are tracks all over the place. Tracks of Bigfoot — half man, half ape," said Francis.

His father laughed above the hum of the water pumps and the cackle of the women feeding freshly washed clothes through the hot rollers of the steaming laundry mangle. "We'll see, Francis. We'll see."

* * *

Francis would be the youngest member of John C. Meehan's campers that summer of 1913. But was he enthusiastic!

The dew-eyed Mr. Meehan fixed his porkpie hat squarely on his head and unbuttoned the top of his Spanish-American War army fatigues. He spied Francis unloading his backpack from his father's 1908 Buick roadster and wondered if the boy would contract the most dangerous of summer camp afflictions, homesickness.

"Good morning Francis. Ready to go?" Mr. Meehan asked the boy as he strode eagerly into the front doors of the YMCA.

"You bet," said Francis, suddenly correcting himself before the deeply reverent youth leader. "I mean, yes, Mr. Meehan."

Although a young man with soft features and hardly a commanding demeanor, Mr. Meehan exuded a presence for which the boys competed. He had a way of looking up to boys, even if they were only half his height.

"Let's go outside and line up for the newspaper fellow," Mr. Meehan said. Twenty boys, two counselors and Mr. Meehan piled out the Taylor Street entrance for their group picture. "Y" camp was big news in 1913.

The Oregonian photographer filled his flash tray with black powder and began assembling the boys on the steps out front. "Keep your packs on and flip up the bills of your hats so I can see your faces," he said. Passersby on the sidewalks stepped around the camera tripod.

One of the boys, Harry Stevens, plopped himself on the lowest row of steps. Three boys slid in beside him with Paul Stone anchoring the other end at Mr. Meehan's feet. Paul, the son of the YMCA's general secretary, adjusted his wire-rimmed glasses and peered into the camera lens.

All the campers wore white sailor hats. Some flipped up the round bills. George Beggs tilted his jauntily on the crown of his head and took a seat next to John McLernan on the top row.

Francis also took his place on the top row of steps. Harrison Huggins sat between him and George. David Foulkes and Herb Foster jostled for their places on the row of steps below Francis. The best baseball player of the bunch, Maurice Bentall, took a seat in the center of the group and tugged down on both ends of his cap until they touched his ears.

Beside Maurice was Harry Beston. To Harry's left sat Lawrence Lockley, the son of the newspaperman. Mr. Meehan pivoted slightly to give Lawrence more room.

The photographer barked at the boys to bunch together on the porch steps.

"Closer! Closer! And quit squirming. Quit wiggling."

"Kaaah-bloo-ey!" the flash powder exploded. A team of horses neighed. One reared back, baring its teeth. The teamster let out a loud oath. Across

Sixth Avenue, the driver of a new-fangled flatbed truck, sputtering under its tightly-strapped load of lumber, craned his neck to see what was happening. Within hours the photographer's film would be transformed into a large picture in the afternoon edition of the newspaper peddled by street corner hawkers in slouch caps. The picture caption would identify the boys this way: "Y.M.C.A. SUMMER CAMPERS WHO WENT TO SPIRIT LAKE, WASH., THIS MORNING."

* * *

"Let's go camping, men," Mr. Meehan said.

Francis and the other boys clambered down the steps and set a quick pace down Taylor Avenue to the harbor. His blanket was rolled neatly around his pack, the way Mr. Meehan had taught him, just like Teddy Roosevelt's Rough Riders on San Juan Hill. He pondered for a moment all the things Mr. Meehan warned him to bring: his comb, hairbrush, toothbrush, a little box with soap in it, and some hiking clothes, the kind that could withstand sharp rocks and prickly blackberry vines.

"Okay boys, right face!" said the camp leader. "Harch!" The crew clunked down the streets to the river dock. Bystanders gawked. Some smirked. Others got out of the boys' way.

John C. Meehan had discovered the scenic beauty of Mount St. Helens on a camping trip in 1909 and was instrumental in getting a special-use permit for a permanent campsite at the south end of the lake in 1911. The first formal boys camp was conducted the following year. The novelty of the adventure had not yet worn off by 1913, not even for Mr. Meehan.

The boys bounded down Taylor Street to the waterfront. Bobbing gently at its berth was the mighty sternwheeler, *Joseph Kellogg.*

"Careful boys, get aboard now, but careful, you hear," said one of the shipmates. "Mighty nice caps you boys got there!"

Francis and his chums swayed this way, then that, as the tightly caulked deck rocked in the current of the Willamette River. Suddenly, it dawned on Francis that he was really embarking on a journey that would take him far away from home, to a place feared by the Indians and rarely visited by white men. Like the other boys around him, Francis felt his legs go rubbery. What spirits awaited?

Slowly, but without hesitation, the *Joseph Kellogg* slipped its moorings and headed downstream to the confluence of the Willamette and Columbia rivers. The summer sun arched overhead towards midday. The skilled pilot in the wheel house of the sternwheeler angled the boat in a northerly direction, down the Columbia's swift current and finally into the onrushing waters of the narrower Cowlitz River, which fed the mighty Columbia.

It would be three full days of travel before Francis would see Spirit Lake. The name conjured up visions of terrified Cowlitz Indians frozen in fear on the banks of a cold lake, aghast at the sight of evil serpents swimming over the surface, snorting steam spouts.

Legend also had it that ancient Douglas firs, flooded by St. Helens' snowmelt to form Spirit Lake hundreds of years earlier, would sometimes mysteriously shed their roots anchoring them to the lake bottom. The trees would explode through the surface of the placid waters beneath icy Mount St. Helens. Francis edged closer to the boys talking about this faraway place called Spirit Lake.

And there was, of course, Bigfoot. What danger lurked in the densely forested reaches of the Toutle River and its tributaries? How would he react to the sight of three-inch-deep footprints of a hairy caveman who survived as his ancestors did in the isolation of Mount St. Helens? How would Bigfoot react to the intrusion of an 11-year-old camper with only a pocketknife to defend himself?

The throbbing engines of the *Joseph Kellogg* pushed the big paddlewheel against the swift current of the Cowlitz. The campers peered into the river brimming with the flow of hundreds of snow-fed creeks and streams. Tomorrow, they would hike up one of those tributaries called the Toutle River, a clear stream whose existence was due to the snowmelt of Mount St. Helens and the spilloff from Spirit Lake.

The *Joseph Kellogg* finally arrived at the town of Kelso on the east bank of the Cowlitz. Longview would not exist for another 13 years. The boys had quieted down during the dreamy boat ride. Now, their eyes opened and their tongues began to roll.

"Where are we? How much farther? Are we almost there?"

"Never you mind," snapped the deckhand directing the gaggle of youth across the gangplank. "Slow down, you apes," he cracked.

Mr. Meehan did not approve of that sort of talk, but he overlooked it for the moment, directing the boys towards the train station a few blocks east.

From across the gangway the boys marched straightaway to the Kelso train depot. There, they clambered aboard an ornate passenger car bound for Castle Rock. None of the boys had ever done anything like this before. By the time the train chugged to a halt in Castle Rock the pitch of the boys' chattering rose again.

"Bring your packs this way and don't dawdle there young fellow," bellowed a grizzled teamster who greeted them at Castle Rock station. The boys would address him as "Mr. Burnside." He helped load the boys' packs into his horse-drawn wagon. His team neighed and danced in place as the boys moseyed around. A couple of guys headed off down the road towards Silver Lake. Pretty soon the other boys fell in behind them on what rumor had it would be a two-day hike. Mr. Burnside's wagon was for the boys' packs and the boxes of food. The campers would walk.

Tromping through the open countryside, the boys occasionally munched at bitter Pacific blackberries, still red and in their buds. It would be another week or two before they would ripen.

Red alder and big-leaf maple clacked in the breeze. Sweat beads on the brows of the hikers gradually disappeared as the sun perched on the hilltops over their shoulders. Time to make camp.

Once again, Mr. Meehan instructed the boys, as he had done back in the "Y" building in downtown Portland, how to cut and notch tree limbs to form the bed frame for their pup tents. Carefully selecting young saplings with fine slender boughs, he demonstrated the art of making a springy mattress over which a canvas cover was stretched taut. Francis soon was tossing in a fitful sleep between his blankets atop his own crude mattress of cedar boughs.

* * *

The next morning, the boys broke camp and resumed their trek into the forest. Francis recalled his father's warnings. Behave. Don't get homesick. And enjoy yourself. He knew he was the youngest. He had something to prove to the YMCA, to Mr. Meehan, to himself. Suddenly, there it was, a huge hornet's nest, as big as a pumpkin in October. Opportunity buzzed.

Some of the boys noticed Francis sauntering towards the hornet's nest. The older boys sensed what he was going to do. Looking over their shoulders, the 14-year-olds picked up their pace with Mr. Meehan far out ahead. Francis gamely picked up a dirt clod the size of a buttermilk biscuit. He unlimbered his arm, held his mouth just so, and then let fly.

"Run for it!" screamed Herb Foster. Paul Stone held his glasses to his nose and lit out down the path. The six boys with Francis ripped down the road, tripping over the exposed roots of a grove of cottonwoods and a minefield of pumiceous stone.

Francis stared wide-eyed a second longer than he should have to admire his aim, dead center. Suddenly, two hornets hit Francis in the forehead, raising welts as big as cat eyes.

Adrenalin pumping, Francis wheeled around and tore out for the group which was now strung out over several hundred yards down the narrowing path to the east.

"Oooooweeee! They got me, they got me!" Francis cried out. Tears blinded him but he held back his sobs. One of the "Y" leaders beckoned Francis to the cool stream. It might have been Mr. Meehan. Francis could not see out of the flood of tears he was trying to contain. The man gently scooped a mudpack from the streambed.

"Naaaah, na-na, na-nah!" the boys taunted Francis.

"Shsss! Get on with your business." It must have been Mr. Meehan. All of the boys hushed. The man ladled three fingers of mud and patted it on Francis' forehead. "This ought to take out some of the sting," he said.

Then the "Y" leader laughed, "You won't forget this trip for a long time, Francis, and we haven't even gotten to the real adventure yet." Francis closed his eyes. He clutched his right hand with his left. The counselor's comment stilled the chattering of the other campers, too. Spirit Lake still lay another day off.

* * *

Dawn broke earlier than the day before. Francis hardly touched his hardtack victuals but drank all of the cocoa the boys referred to as their choc-coffee. They broke camp and trotted off towards St. Helens. Today, they would see Spirit Lake.

The boys closed ranks as the 300-year-old firs closed in around them. They had been on the trail three days. They were sweaty. Tired. Especially the younger ones.

Drunkards must have blazed the winding path through the forest of old-growth fir and cedar. Francis sipped a mouthful of icy water from a silvery loop of a stream. The timber grew taller and taller even though the nutrient-poor volcanic soil made survival a struggle. Nobody would remember who saw it first. It happened in a sudden. There, shimmering under a cool, cloudless sky, was Spirit Lake.

A log cabin owned by Mr. and Mrs. E.S. Collins faced the lake to the north towards the outlet. Francis and the boys hiked around past the cabin to the Spirit Lake boys' camp. Camp Blister. There were no buildings. Only tents. Tonight, however, there would be no complaints. Fatigue swept over the campers' exultation. It was time for deep, impenetrable sleep. Even Bigfoot would have a hard time waking the boys this evening.

Chapter IV

The Hairy Apes of Mount St. Helens

D awn's first light peeked over the Dogs Head glacier of Mount St. Helens and skipped across the choppy wavelets of Spirit Lake. A growl from Amos Lawrence's stomach awakened the boy from his slumber. Hunger gnawed deep inside.

Suddenly, without warning, a boy armed with a bugle blasted a few bars of reveille, shattering the stillness of morning. Dozens of sleepy-eyed campers burst forth from their two-man, shelter-half tents, scurrying about half-dressed. Some headed for the latrine, others for the maniacal plunge into Spirit Lake, if it had not iced over during the night.

"Yeeee-hah!" they screamed murderously. One dive under was usually enough. Then, splashing for dear life, they dashed back to their tents to dress and line up outside the mess hall for flapjacks and choc-coffee.

Amos met up with big Paul Bale, square-shouldered and hefty, who though also 14 years of age was bigger than Amos.

"I'm hungry," said Amos.

"Me too," agreed Paul.

The philosophy of the camp staff seemed to be to keep the boys hungry, ravenously hungry. Anything they ate tasted swell. There was sailor's hard-

21

tack, sometimes moldy, always hard. And raisins, canned salmon, canned pork and beans, Tillamook cheese, peanuts and canned pineapple chunks. And of course, Hershey bars mailed to camp from the folks back home or purchased in the camp store. The only thing that could top a camper's cup brimming with snow and pineapple chunks was a brittle block of Hershey's almond chocolate.

"I'll trade you for that Hershey bar, the one with almonds," Amos said to Paul. Chocolate bars were the currency of exchange at the YMCA summer camp on Spirit Lake in 1924.

"What'll you gimme?"

"Wait a minute. You've already eaten part of it," said Amos.

"Not that much," said Paul.

Two other boys joined Paul and Amos. Both 14, they were Jimmy Babson, another big-shouldered lad, and Bob Sellers, a tumbler and gymnast. Together, the four rising freshmen at Grant High School in Portland made a crew known throughout camp for their prowess and devotion to physical fitness. Like others in camp, they were working their way up from leisurely backcountry hikes to Mount Margaret and Meta Lake to more strenuous climbs along the ridges of Mount St. Helens itself.

"Morning boys. Today you're going to do the Around-the-Mountain hike, I hear," said a tall man of six feet or so. Mr. Meehan, the softspoken camp director, was a person of quiet demeanor who commanded the boys' respect. His piercing eyes transfixed the campers.

"Yes sir, Mr. Meehan," said Amos in the respectful tone he reserved for John C. Meehan, the founder of the YMCA camp 13 years earlier. Amos had long known of Mr. Meehan from his brothers, Denny, who attended camp during the summers of 1920 to 1923, and Abbott, who attended the summers of 1919 and 1920. Mr. Meehan's remarks were always guarded, never intending to hurt, positive, always reinforcing. He led camp prayers at meals and spoke of the Great Spirit at campfires.

Mr. Meehan promoted physical fitness, especially in the form of hikes that culminated in a climb to the pinnacle of 9,677-foot Mount St. Helens. That was his style: set objectives, then urge the boys to achieve those goals.

"Well, get on in to breakfast then. Flapjacks today. Amos, you should save that candy bar for the trail when you might need it," Mr. Meehan added.

* * *

Amos untied the ropes to his half of the tent and rolled the canvas tightly. Then he rolled his blanket and slung it diagonally across his shoulders as he had seen Spanish-American War veterans do in picture history books.

All that was left on the ground was the notched log frame with fir boughs that had been his mattress the past few nights.

Tonight, he and his mates would sleep on the east side of Mount St. Helens at the very top of Thousand Foot Canyon, later to become known as "Ape Canyon."

The boys hiked out of camp around Spirit Lake, glistening in the already hot sun of mid-July. At 3,200 feet in elevation, Timberline Trail took the breath of most first-time hikers. But on this morning the campers moved out quickly, setting a feverish pace. They had already hardened themselves with dozens of lesser climbs. Besides, the eastside trek was their favorite test of endurance.

Squad Leader Sam Lockwood urged his charges onward toward the 4,000-foot level and then through Windy Pass at 5,000 feet. There would be no turning back now as the tree line faded below. Amos unwrapped his chocolate bar and bit off a piece. It was melting. No need to repackage it and ruin his shirt. Amos passed the bar around to Paul.

"Here, for some Lionel Strongfart muscle-power!" he said, perverting the name of a then-popular muscle man whose amazing bodybuilding secrets were sold through an ad in the back of a boy's magazine. Paul took the bar and laughed, flexing his bicep for all to see.

Mr. Lockwood cleared his throat. The boys' prattle ceased.

They did not fear Mr. Lockwood. Rather they respected the counselor. He was always exhorting them to finish the most grueling hikes without a whimper. It was Mr. Lockwood, after all, who had pushed and encouraged Amos to finish his hike up Mount Margaret a week earlier. All in, Amos would not have made it without Mr. Lockwood's encouragement.

Mr. Lockwood strode briskly today, testing the boys' endurance. A turbulent sea of clouds boiled in the Cascade valleys below. Stratus clouds reflected sunrise pinks and reds, silhouetting Mount Adams to the east and the brawny Mount Rainier far to the north.

The trail gradually spilled into Abraham Flat, a half-mile wide shelf at the 5,000 foot level of Mount St. Helens. Pumice Butte—called Pumy Hill by a decade of "Y" campers — was within sight. Stands of pine, hemlock and Douglas fir peered up at the boys from the mountainside. All morning they passed through pockets of wildflowers and Pacific lupine, patches of huckleberries and hearty little alpine trees. But even the heartiest species of shrubs and trees seemed to cringe at this elevation, bent and humbled by the short growing season, the paucity of nutrients in the soil and the violent swings in temperature.

"Why isn't anything growing around here?" one of the boys asked.

Mr. Lockwood picked at a tuft of bear hair, a puff-ball of black stringy grass, and said, "There are things growing here. You have to look hard. But the main reason you don't have any trees right here is that St. Helens sweeps the slopes clean with avalanches every year."

Paul and Jimmy craned their necks skyward at the peak, suddenly capped now in a bewildering swirl of clouds.

"Oh boy, I bet old George is cussing now," said Amos.

Bob Sellers chortled at the thought of George Schnitgler — the U.S. Forest Service's "man on the mountain." It was his job to spot forest fires from the little summit lookout station constructed seven years earlier in 1917 on the very pinnacle of Mount St. Helens. When the haze and bad weather closed in on the reinforced cabin with glass-enclosed cupola, old George could hardly see his hand in front of his face, much less spot forest fires in the valleys far below. And, of course, when it was clear on the summit, chances were great that the valleys below were socked in, obscuring any potential telltale ribbons of smoke.

"Yeah, no wonder he cusses so," Amos replied. Paul and Jimmy laughed. Mr. Lockwood repressed a grin and kept up the pace as the noonday sun beat down on the squad. George Schnitgler's colorful use of the English language, and some other tongues, was well known.

While his forest fire spotting was subject to review, Mr. Schnitgler's service as an eccentric character in numerous climbing legends was beyond dispute. He was a fiery, red-haired, blue-eyed, mountain man, attired in pegged work jeans, cuffed logger-style a full six inches from the top of his boots. His pants were slick with cooking grease. Bulbous nose, bushy eyebrows, receding hairline with a permanently windblown look, he was a big man. His smile reflected an ever-present contentment from all the sunrises and sunsets he had seen through the sights of the firefinder there in his tiny lookout on top of the world.

Amos could hardly wait until the day he would meet Mr. Schnitgler. On his first ascent of Mount St. Helens, Amos hoped he would be treated to Mr. Schnitgler's specialty, hot coffee and homemade donuts. The thought helped Amos keep up with Mr. Lockwood's now furious pace towards the Plains of Abraham.

Dust devils whipped up around the boys' legs. Panting, they slogged through eight inches of pumice deposited 124 years earlier by an eruption of St. Helens. In between their complaints of fatigue, the boys pelted each other with pumy stones the size of their fingertips to keep the hike lively. The day drifted on into cool evening as they traversed the flattening terrain. They speculated on the cougar—or was it a black bear?—darting among the stand of Noble fir far, far down below.

At last, Mr. Lockwood halted the column. The 6,500-foot climatological timberline limit was clearly visible above them. The squad made camp on the tree-covered banks of a stream fed by the flour-white flows off St. Helens' glaciers high above. Several boys sat on bunch grass and nipped with pocketknives at tender boughs from nearby saplings to make their mattresses.

Mr. Lockwood began dinner, his thoughts drifting towards vespers. When Amos and his pals finished pitching their pup tents, they dawdled around camp. Hunger gnawed at them. Their conversation turned to pork and beans. However ungrand beans sounded, there would be no complaints.

"Why don't you guys go for a hike? Go look down Thousand Foot Canyon," Mr. Lockwood suggested since dinner was still 15 minutes away.

"Yeah, let's go," cried Jimmy, breaking for the clearing down which the trail would lead the four boys to a narrow canyon on the southeast side of the mountain.

Amos and Paul bolted camp behind Bob Sellers who was gaining on Jimmy by the time they lurched to a halt on the dangerous precipice at the highest point atop the canyon.

Bob intentionally bumped Jimmy, good-naturedly, as if to push him over the edge. Jimmy pushed back: "Hey!"

Amos and Paul slid into the clearing, pumiceous dust clouds swirling all around them.

"Hey! Look at me!" cried Paul as he picked up a pumy stone the size of a basketball. He deftly flipped it off the cliff. "I'm Lionel Strongfaaaart — the strongest man on the mountain!" he said, flexing again both biceps for the other three boys to admire.

"Oh yeah, me too!" Amos yelled as he picked up a great stone the size and weight of an empty orange crate. He flung it off the cliff with seemingly massive exertion of his upper torso, grunted, then spun around in search of another stone.

Bob added his own gymnastic twists to flinging two pumy rocks over the cliff, both of them arching high and distant into the unknown below.

Big-shouldered Jimmy Babson imitated a gorilla, hunching over and dragging his knuckles on the ground until he clutched a particularly huge pumy boulder, teetered under its weight and tossed it over the edge. Then he yelled, a chilling howl that echoed across the canyon.

"Yaaaaah-eeeeeh-ohaaaa!"

Amos, Paul and Bob did likewise, slipping in the scree and boasting their power and strength — "as strong as Lionel Strongfaaaart!"

* * *

A boy of 10 or so dipped his bucket into Smith Creek and headed back into Thousand Foot Canyon towards a splintery old miner's cabin. The coffee would taste good with dinner this cool evening after such a long, warm day hauling rocks. That was his job, hauling rocks and debris chipped out of the mine being dug by his uncle and another man. The three were holing up that summer of 1924 in a sparse cabin at the foot of the great crevasse of Thousand Foot Canyon for one reason: Gold.

They had panned Smith Creek, chipped away at a hundred dead-end veins and were a bit down on their luck. Not even a sign of copper, much less some rarer metal.

The boy trudged back through the fine rock and ash that blew off the mountain. His uncle would probably be nipping at the bottle by now. So would his partner.

Suddenly, there was a piercing cry followed by a resounding thud.

"Aaaaah-aaaaah-aaaaah! Thum-bum-buuum!"

Then another cry.

"Oooh-aaaaah!"

Followed by another gut-wrenching impact.

"Kaaah-wum-bum-buuum!"

The boy hurried through the prickly currant patch out of the sunshine and into a tangle of sword ferns. A furry pocket gopher dove for cover as the boy tripped over a chunk of granite. His pail of water splashed across the path.

"Aaaaah-ooooh-aaaaah!" came an echo down the canyon.

The boy looked up the path directly into the V-section of Thousand Foot Canyon at the bottom of which stood the rickety old cabin with a tin roof. He caught sight of a gigantic boulder flying through the air. It floated a moment then struck the side of the cliff before crashing into the rubble at the base about fifty yards from the cabin.

"Kaaah-buuum!"

Glancing upward, the boy glimpsed a hunched-over, two-legged creature dragging yet another boulder the size of a dog house. The broad-shouldered creature carefully toed the precipice. Then he stood upright like a big hairy gorilla with the boulder suspended high above his shaggy head. The beast let out an angry growl followed by a ghoulish yell, then tossed the stone effortlessly into the canyon, narrowly missing the stovepipe chimney on the rear of the cabin.

The boy sprang to his feet and dashed the 50 yards or so to the cabin door. The latch was up, the door slightly ajar.

"Haw-wham!" the door flew back on its hinges as the boy burst through the opening. His uncle was napping on the bunk in the corner. His partner was nodding over a yellowing copy of *The Oregonian*. Both men snapped open their eyes as if to suggest that there had better be a good explanation for the ruckus.

"Monsters, monsters!" the boy yelled hysterically. He pointed outside towards the canyon walls. "Some monsters are going to get us! Quick, come see," the boy shouted.

His uncle cocked his elbow on the mattress and stroked his chin. He had heard some commotion outside but had given it no mind. His thoughts were on the traces of ore found earlier that morning. He was celebrating with his partner, pondering whether to continue prospecting through the summer. Now this. Monsters!

The partner looked at the boy, skeptical of what he was hearing but also somewhat amused. The boy was sure excitable.

"You don't say?" the partner egged on the boy.

"Yeah, yeah, ya' hear? They're coming to get us right now," the boy sputtered. His eyes bulged out of their sockets.

His uncle sat up on the bunk. "Now suppose you just describe these big beasts to your old uncle," he said with a wink towards his half-tight partner.

"They was big, hairy, like gorillas," the boy shot back.

"Did they walk on all fours and chase sticks like Laddie here?" the partner asked as he reached down and petted an ancient red-haired collie with a trace of Irish setter.

"No, no. They walked hunched over and then stood up on their hind legs, just like you or me," the boy said.

The two men laughed at the boy's antics. "Well, you seen a bear," said his uncle. "You seen a black bear, I betcha, a'walkin' around the huckleberry patch by Smith Creek down below." He reached over and took another swallow from a wine bottle sitting on the table.

The boy refused to have his story dismissed so casually. Even while his uncle and his partner laughed, the boy trembled at his recollection of his attackers.

"They weren't bears. I've seen bears. They weren't bears. Bears have snouts and fur on their faces. These were monsters, I tell you. They had big shoulders and mean faces with hairy bodies but you could still see their hands. Their HANDS! They had hands — bears don't have hands!"

The laughter of the two men sort of faded.

"Hands, you say?" said the partner. He held up his own open palm before the boy. Then he scratched the back of his head.

"Yeah, only hairy. A lot bigger. And stronger. Big enough to pick up the wagon outside," the boy replied.

The partner looked at the boy's uncle. He let out a laugh. The boy's uncle snorted, ran his hand through his hair and stroked his chin, thoughtfully. "And they're comin' to git us, right?"

"Unc, they was up top Thousand Foot Canyon, way up there. I saw 'em throwing rocks down at me, rocks as big as this house, well, almost as big. And they was yellin', like they was mad at us for bein' here or something."

His uncle chuckled softly, incredulously. "Well," he said to his partner, "I guess we had better have a look-see," and strode through the open door.

"Don't! Don't! They'll get you Unc!" the boy pleaded. Genuine terror in the boy's eyes startled the partner. He paused.

"Maybe the boy did see something. Only I bet it was just a mama bear with her cubs."

"T'wasn't a bear, I'm tellin' ya," the boy said. His uncle looked over his shoulder at his partner. He was not smiling now. Indeed, he looked a bit concerned. "Let's get to the bottom of this."

The boy's uncle walked outside, wandered around the cabin clearing and then peered up the canyon to the highest reaches. For a moment, he thought he saw something move, something resembling a dark hairy head disappearing under the low bough of a massive fir tree. The wind was picking up. It must have been the wind.

His partner ambled around the cabin. "See anything?"

"Naw, the boy's imagining things," he said. "Probably them "Y" campers."

"No I'm not. Look'it over there at all that dust flying around where they flung them boulders," the boy said, pointing to the smoking rubble nearby. Shadows from the setting sun were creeping up the sides of the canyon walls but the telltale clouds of dust were readily apparent, even to the boy's doubters. Tonight would be a long one for the miners.

* * *

Bob Lambert swept the toast crumbs from his breakfast off the tabletop and reconnoitered the office for the most recent issue of *The Oregonian*. No longer was there a need for a fire in the woodstove. The morning sun was heating up the firewatch station just fine. Lambert preferred this duty to that of logging in the cold and squishy timberlands around his former home of Toledo. Together with his partner, Rant Mullins, they comprised the U.S. Forest Service's "Saturday staff" at the Spirit Lake station in July, 1924.

While rain spoils many a weekend in Oregon and Washington, nature had blessed Mount St. Helens this summer with a dry spell. That meant lots of tourists and lots of fires caused by their carelessness. Thus, the need for fire duty this particular Saturday morning.

Lambert did not mind fire watch though. He was a storyteller and the tourists and the frisky young apes at the nearby YMCA camp always made enthusiastic audiences for him. Lambert called all kids "apes," a term of endearment left over from his logging days.

"Bob, there's a bunch of guys headin' in from the southeast," Rant said.

Lambert stopped his sweeping and looked out the window.

He swigged his cup of coffee and peered through the forest clearing at the approaching strangers. They appeared to be in a hurry. Two men and a little ape, 10 or 12 years old. He looked scared.

"Howdy!" Mullins waved to the group. They said nothing, approaching instead the front porch of the ranger station with a sense of urgency.

"What's wrong, gents?" Lambert asked, for there was no question that this crew was perturbed.

"We've got a problem. Seems somebody's throwin' rocks, big boulders I mean to say, down Thousand Foot Canyon," said the older of the miners.

"Yeah, onto our cabin!" snapped his partner. "You know the cabin there at the foot of the canyon? Well, the boy seen 'em that was doing it, way up there on top. We didn't believe him at first, but then come to find the whole side of our shed out back caved in. We think it was them YMCA boys."

"Oh, I think maybe some apes threw them down on you, all right. Haven't you heard of the apes up there? The apes roll those rocks down," Lambert said.

The two miners rocked back on their heels at the mention of the word "apes." The boy smiled and said, "See, I told ya' I'd seen something that warn't human."

"Well, what do you think we ought to do?" the older of the two miners asked Lambert.

Lambert stepped aside as Mullins climbed the porch steps. He looked up at the suddenly brooding sky and casually mentioned, "I don't know, but I doubt that it'd be too smart to tangle with those apes. Nope. Not smart at all. Besides, looks like we may be in for a drenching before you get back to your cabin. You probably ought to hole up at the campground tonight."

The miners looked at the sky and then at one another, taken aback by Lambert's revelation. They ambled away from the ranger station towards the campground, mumbling just out of earshot about the weather and their close encounter with the hairy apes of Mount St. Helens.

The weather tended to change quickly around Spirit Lake. Indeed, Mount St. Helens created its own weather. One moment, birds twitter among tree branches bathed in sunshine. Blink twice though and the wind will kick up out of the southeast and blow down a sky full of black clouds that fill up the green valleys and totally obscure the sun.

"Looks like we might not have to worry about fires in 'Ape Canyon' today," Lambert said over his shoulder to Mullins.

* * *

Later that evening, Lambert and Mullins gathered around the wood stove, recounting the ape tale told to the miners. A third forester, Bill Allen, was holding his sides from laughter.

"Well," Allen asked, "what are ya' going to do for an encore?"

"I don't know if he needs an encore after his performance this afternoon, Bill. I'm tellin' ya', those miners turned white at the mention of 'those apes.' "

"I'm sure it was just those "Y" camp apes," said Lambert.

"But you would have thought it was the bogeyman of 'Ape Canyon' from the terrible look in those bloodshot eyes of his," Mullins said of the older miner.

"I do have an encore in mind," Lambert said. There was a moment of silent expectation.

"I'm going to really put the fear of apes in those miners' hearts," said Lambert. Then he pulled out a large pair of wooden sandals the shape of feet. Big feet. The sandals had straps around them so he could wear them over his own boots.

"You boys come with me if you want a real good laugh," said Lambert.

With that, the three sneaked off down the hill through the chilly night air to the "official" boat of the U.S. Forest Service. The "official-ness" of the boat was a joke, of course, since it was merely a rowboat of dubious sea-worthiness. Mullins wrapped some rags around the oarlocks to keep the squeaky rowing to a minimum. Allen settled into the seat in the bow while Lambert shoved off and jumped into the stern. There, he pulled on his Bigfoot shoes and laced up the straps.

"Fellas, I do believe those apes must have followed the miners down to the campground," Lambert chortled.

The trip across the lake went smoothly. There was a lot of activity all around Spirit Lake. John C. Meehan would have his YMCA campers spell-bound around the dying embers of their campfire. The flickering candles and warm lantern lights identifying cabins isolated here and there along the lake were beginning to die out one by one as the lodgers retired. Old George Schnitgler was sure to be cozy by now in the fire lookout cabin on the summit of Mount St. Helens.

The yellow embers of a dozen fires scattered throughout the nearly full campground flickered in the night. The miners' tents were dark. Allen waited for the bow of the boat to nudge the sandy shoreline before he jumped out and yanked on the rope. He muffled his snickering. Mullins decided to stay put in the boat, oars at the ready in case the three had to make a hasty departure. "Be careful, Bigfoot," he said to Lambert as he stepped lightly out of the boat.

A full moon darted in and out of feathery black clouds. It was dark, but not so dark that Lambert could not see his way around the miners' camp. He looked out of the corners of his eyes for guywires over which he might trip. Many alpine hikers were in the area for the weekend.

A fresh rain that afternoon made the spongy soil impressionable. Lambert treaded heavily up to the fireplace tripods, then back around to the doors of the miners' tents and out towards a dilapidated outhouse. Everywhere he walked, Lambert left his Bigfoot prints deeply pressed into the ground.

"Hurry up," Mullins cried out hoarsely, barely able to contain his laughter.

Lambert laughed too. "The deed's done. Let's go. Tomorrow, people are going to be asking me if it's Bigfoot," Lambert guffawed.

"What are you going to say to 'em?" Mullins asked.

Lambert broke into a broad grin: "I'm going to say, 'Yeah, it sure is a big footprint!' "

Chapter V

Lige Coalman's Farewell
to Spirit Lake

Summer was nearing an end. It was the last day at "Y" camp and rumors crackled like wildfire in dry brush. Curtis and Randy and their two cabin mates, Ted and Sam, had never been to the Portland YMCA summer camp until that summer of 1937. Now, word had it that the camp was losing Lige Coalman, the mountain man, and might not reopen next year.

"Just when I was thinking about climbing the mountain!" said Curtis.

"Why close it anyway?" asked Randy.

"They aren't gonna let kids run it by themselves. Mr. Coalman is a'leaving. Who could replace him?" replied Sam.

The four boys, all of them 12 years old, strolled from their cabin to Holmstedt Lodge. A fire crackled behind the andirons of the huge fireplace at the end of the cavernous building. Fifty guests could sleep in the lodge, but this morning it was quiet. The four boys shuffled across the floor to the dying embers to ward off the chill that Saturday morning.

A tall man, 56 years old, wearing a worn and wrinkled blue chambray work shirt and old brown trousers with red suspenders walked in the back door. Cradled in his right arm was a load of bright red alder. The heavy load brought out the sharp trenchwork of wrinkles across his forehead. He had crow's-feet

33

stamped on his temples that seemed to lock his eyes in a squint. Lige Coalman ambled towards the fireplace, oblivious to the boys' deafening silence.

"What're you guys up to? You packed up?"

"Yes sir," snapped Curtis.

"Well, the truck ought to be here in a while. You guys ought to hike out to the lake trail. Get a view of Mount St. Helens one more time."

"You mean one last time, don'tcha?" said the usually silent Sam.

Coalman balanced the firewood with his right hand and fed the blaze with his left. Without looking at him, he asked Sam, "Aren't you coming back next year, Sam?"

"Well, yes sir, that is if they have camp next year."

"Sure we will. Why wouldn't we have "Y" camp next summer?"

All four boys blurted their fears: "But we heard you was leavin'. We heard they were shutting down the camp. Who'd run it without you?"

Coalman flicked the last chunk of alder onto the fire, which roared from the draft of the open lodge door. He chortled.

"I'm leaving, that's true enough. But this YMCA camp's going to continue right on in 1938, boys. I'm not the Portland YMCA all by myself. I'm not the only leader. Things will go on just fine without me here to keep Mount St. Helens in line." He smiled, then stood up to his full height, towering over the boys.

"Why are you leaving, Mr. Coalman? Where are you going?"

"Oh, to another YMCA camp that needs some help down in California. And why? Well, I guess the real question you ought to know the answer to is why I came here to Spirit Lake in the first place."

"Why did you?"

Coalman turned towards the boys, his backside to the fire.

"I joined the Portland "Y" staff in 1925. It was natural I was asked to come here the following year because I'm pretty good with a hammer and I know my way around the woods. I'm not averse to washing the dishes, either."

The boys laughed with Coalman, but quickly cross-examined him: "Come on, Mr. Coalman, why'd you come up here?"

"I guess I came here to build character in my own boys and in boys like you. I've done a lot of things, you all know that. But nothing's as important to me as seeing young saplings sink deep roots and grow strong enough to withstand a gale.

"We've got some time, I suppose. I'll tell you some stories, if you like, that will explain to you how I got the way I am."

"Oh yesss! Please do, Mr. Coalman," the boys shouted back.

"I was born back in the last century in 1881 at the foot of Mount Hood in a log cabin built by my father, Stephen Coalman.

"Those were rugged days. I know that when I was just a baby, my folks took me to Government Camp on Mount Hood to pick huckleberries. My parents ended up burying a little baby only slightly younger than me."

"What happened to the baby, Mr. Coalman?" asked one of his wide-eyed charges.

"Oh, we were staying with our good friend, Perry Vickers, at his lodge called the Summit House. We took the downstairs bedroom. That night, the two-month old Barclay baby took to crying and moaning. My mother went outside to the immigrant parents' tent and did what she could, but it was no use.

"My father ended up building a coffin for the Barclay baby. Perry Vickers allowed the burial of that baby right outside the Summit House the next day. I'll tell you something else.

"Ten years later, they buried Perry beside the Barclay baby after a thief he had tried to arrest shot Perry in the stomach with a Sharp's rifle at near point-blank range. The only reason I tell you this horrible fact is that I admired Perry Vickers. He influenced my whole life. He was the first white man I know of to see the sun set one night and rise the next morning from the pinnacle of Mount Hood. He was a climber, a woodsman, a spiritual man who wrote poetry. He even once swam the Salmon River with me in a papoose strapped to his back."

Coalman paused for the realization to sink in to the boys' consciousness.

"My mother Elizabeth Harnett Coalman died eighteen months after I was born, right after father built her a new, bigger cabin.

"My father was superintendent of the Barlow Toll Road: $2.50 for a team, $1.25 for a saddle horse, six cents each for cattle and four for sheep. He was always busy repairing the bridges over the 25 stream crossings and helping out wayward pioneers. He didn't have much time for me but he loved me and that's what's important.

"I had some other good influences, too. After my mother died, my father worked it so some neighbors raised me right along with their own nine children. Steve and Ellen Mitchell—good folks. I lacked for nothing, though I'll tell you boys, my upbringing was different from yours.

"We threshed wheat by hand, had it ground into bran, shorts, middlings and white flour at a German miller's gristmill two miles down the road.

"We grew our corn, shelled it by hand, and slaughtered our own cattle or hogs, sheep or poultry, when we wanted meat."

Curtis had heard Coalman's story about his father killing a bear, so he asked, "How about wild game, Mr. Coalman?"

"Oh sure, elk, deer and bear, raccoons too. My favorites have always been trout and salmon, fresh, dried or smoked. And berries too, fresh, canned, preserved, jellied or jammed. We had all the honey we wanted, straight from the wild bee trees. You could get three and a half washbasins of honey from a bee tree.

"My upbringing strengthened me. I had to rely on myself a lot. But I was a weakling until Mrs. Foster started a Sunday school when I was about your age, boys. We met in Fred Hatch's store building there in Sandy. Mrs. Foster's lessons opened my eyes to the Lord."

Coalman let the word sink in.

"You need inner strength, you need moral fiber. You're going to see a lot that isn't right as you grow up. You've got to recognize right from wrong and have the courage to face cold reality even when it's not pretty.

"I remember as a boy riding into Sandy on a buckboard wagon with my father one day. We came upon a scene I dream about even today. We saw a deputy sheriff unleash both barrels of a shotgun into the chest of a horse thief in flight from The Dalles. The force of the double-blast flipped the thief over backwards.

"My father jumped out of the wagon, leaving me to hold the reins. He helped carry the thief to the porch where they covered him with a flap of canvas. In a few minutes, he was dead. I wake up at night from the gruesome memory of his back flip, but the man was guilty and the deputy was exonerated for the self-defense shooting. My father was the prosecutor's chief witness."

The boys around Coalman were entranced and did not move as he reached over for the fire poker and shook out the hot coals. Sparks flew up the chimney.

"Where do you get courage, Mr. Coalman?" asked Sam. The others added a chorus of "Yeah? How did you get so brave?"

Coalman let out a loud laugh. "It comes with practice, I guess." He grinned, then realized the boys wanted more. "I only went through fourth grade, so I taught myself to read at higher levels. One night when I was 12, I was reading by the fireplace when we heard one of our pigs squeal. Father thought the dogs were fighting, but then he said, 'Something's got hold of one of the hogs.' We both bolted through the cabin door into the night.

"I carried the lantern and raised it high so my father could see what it was. He grabbed a loose fence rail, eight feet long, and peered across the dark pig sty at a great black bear backing over the far side of the fence with his teeth sunk in the back of the hog's neck.

"Father made a great swing with the fence rail. The bear balanced himself with his left paw and leg. He kept hold of that pig with his teeth and swiped at the swinging fence rail with his right paw. The rail swung back, struck me in the shoulder and knocked the lantern from my hands. The globe flipped up and the breeze blew out our light. I lay on the ground fully convinced I had been completely killed. One of our dogs leaped at the bear, but he knocked him back into a yelping spasm that was little short of terrifying.

"All the dogs took up the cry. The pig squealed louder. My father raised that fence rail for another swipe at the bear's snout: 'Drop that pig! Drop that pig!' he yelled. Incredibly, the bear did drop it and fled into the night."

The four boys laughed. Coalman shook his head, grinning broadly. "Of course, courage isn't just beating a bear over the head with a fence rail. It's having good sense and the willingness to use it.

"I remember one time one of my friends, a boy named Tom Paine, was going hunting with his father. I wanted to go, too, but father wouldn't let me. He told me, 'Tom Paine Senior is a careless man. He doesn't ever mean to be, but he shoots his gun too fast. He talks too loud and too much, sometimes about things he doesn't really know about. He goes hunting for deer and bear, just for the fun of shooting them, when he doesn't really need the meat. He is a very lucky man because he has such a fine wife who believes in God and loves her husband and their son. Young Tom Junior is a fine boy and I'm glad you play with him, but I don't want you to go hunting or fishing or out in the woods with him and his father.' "

Coalman bowed his head.

"Tom Paine shot Tommy in the stomach that day. Oh, it was an accident. He thought the movement in the brush was a deer, but it was his son.

"The husky Copper boys, neighbors of ours, helped father and Tom Paine carry the stretcher with Tommy crying and asking for water. They gave it to him and it seemed to ease his pain for a time. Suddenly he began to scream again and flail his arms. Then he stiffened and was dead."

The four boys looked at one another. Coalman's instructive stories were rarely ambiguous. All summer long, Lige Coalman had been exhorting "Y" campers to excel, respect nature and do the right thing.

His reputation as a life saver throughout the wilderness was legendary, and his message was also plain: Serve others and you serve yourself. Ted turned to Curtis and asked in an aside if he had heard the story about the time when Coalman was 17 and saved a man's life. He gaffed the drowning man by the back of his shirt, yanked him from the Sandy River and still had time to catch 62 salmon before night fell.

Curtis murmured back to Ted that he had heard that story. In the same breath though he asked, "Mr. Coalman, how many times did you climb Mount Hood?"

Mountaineering was his favorite subject. Coalman said, "I think 586 times, more or less. Each climb was memorable. Each was dangerous, of course. But the number doesn't really matter, Curtis. It's not the accomplishment of conquering a mountain that matters, so much. It's the privilege you experience when you can be there to see God's handiwork. Of all the animals, we human beings are the only ones that can realize the significance of the sunrise or the glory of a sunset.

"We kill deer to stock our larders. We chop wood to fuel our stoves. We fell big timber to build our cabins. And I guess I climbed my share of mountains just to add another notch to the list or make $5 as a mountain guide. But I've never forgotten the reason God put me on this earth. To serve Him.

"I'll tell you one last story, then you boys better go grab your grip. The truck is coming now, I can hear it.

"Back in 1915, Bruce Osborne, head of the lookout division of the forest service, called on me to establish the first fire lookout on the summit of Mount Hood. I was the old man of the mountain, the most experienced guide around, but still it was an honor he would call me.

"We toted supplies and whatnot, and we laid a telephone line for our field phone to the very pinnacle. We reached the summit at 2 p.m., July 21, and placed a phone call 30 minutes later to Portland. Now isn't that amazing?"

The boys all said, "Yeaaah!"

"Well, in a small way, it was kind of entertaining and kind of an accomplishment. But let me tell you, we stayed up there that windy night in our tied-down tent, praying we wouldn't be blown 4,000 feet into Eliot Glacier. I figured out that night that man's little triumphs are nothing compared to what is routine for the Lord.

"The next day was a beautiful morning with no wind. We got out early enough to witness the sunrise and it was then I first felt as though the spirit of Perry Vickers, that first man to sleep at the top and write poetry about it, was standing beside me. A sunrise or a sunset from the top of a mountain is the treat of a lifetime. I witnessed dozens during the following four summers until I left in 1919. The glory of each sunrise and each sunset varied by the brush stroke of God's artistry.

"I want you boys to climb Mount St. Helens next summer when you come back here to Spirit Lake. I want you to see what I've seen and really feel it. I'll be with you in spirit. Now get your belongings together. The truck is waiting for your squad now."

Chapter VI

The High Society of Spirit Lake

Harmony Falls Lodge with its coterie of cabin owners was a class apart from the rest of the Spirit Lake community. With their bucket privies and oil lamp-lit theaters, the high spirited society made itself the arbiter of Spirit Lake fashion and values . . . for at least one week a year.

The lodge itself anchored six acres of lakeside flatland on the north end of Spirit Lake. At one time, 11 cabins surrounded the great building. All faced south where Mount St. Helens rose out of the horizon just above the end of the lake.

Behind the lodge where the tall timber began, Harmony Creek burst over a rock outcropping, splashing down in a 100-foot, white bridal veil blurred by a column of swirling mist. The creek flowed through the resort to Spirit Lake. Little bridges crisscrossed the creek. In the fall, lucky guests could watch the waters ripple with the primordial shadows of Coho salmon spawning in the shallows shortly after a heavy rain.

Farther back in the woods was remote Tree Top. A tiny, timberbound cabin high up a steep path, Tree Top was impractical for guests toting a lot of gear. Lodge staff dreaded hauling wood to it and joked they needed to "rope up" to get there. Tree Top fell into disuse and a heavy snowfall finished it off one winter. Shortly thereafter, Tree Top faded into a memory.

Melody Hut, Paddle Inn, the Lookout, Harmony Hums and Shangri-La clustered around the stream fed by Harmony Falls. Cottonwoods flourished when youngsters were persuaded not to swing on them.

On the edge of the lake the Gov'ners Mansion, with its exposed two-by-four framing and leaky shake roof, guarded the floating dock used for swimming.

Many a couple, young and old alike, were mesmerized by the sunsets from the deck of Harmony Falls' smallest cabin, the Eagle's Roost, perched on stilts overlooking the lake. From here St. Helens loomed large on the horizon, a happy presence that begged to be photographed.

North of the lodge and adjacent to the Malarkey family cabin was another rustic dwelling called Harmony Fails. The name was apt when the wind and rain poured through holes in the roof.

The daily rates were $10 and up for a double occupancy cabin, and $20 and up for a large. Included in the price was boat fare from the southwestern side of the lake where the road stopped. Harmony Falls Lodge was hidden from view across the lake on the northeastern shoreline, too far for a family with luggage to hike. Fortunately, there was an ancient, handcrank telephone on a tree to yell "We're here! Come get us, please." Lodge proprietor Jack Nelson would be over in a moment, piloting one of the launches, the *Tressa* or the *Ruby*. You could back your family station wagon right down the end of the road onto the dock and load your suitcases and duffel bags right into the boat.

After loading, Nelson would ease his boat away from shore and putt-putt across the lake a quarter of a mile while his guests chattered about what was new. Suddenly, a hand would point and a voice cry out, "Look!" Quietly, with renowned stealth, the creamy white glaciers of Mount St. Helens appeared above the pointy tops of ancient evergreens. Until this moment, St. Helens had always been a distant view. Suddenly, it dominated the skyline.

The comparatively high cabin rates were not for fancy accoutrements or lodge services. Rather, the cost covered what guests did not get: Phone service, traffic, noise, television. In short, civilization as we know it. Each cabin had its own woodstove, a couple of oil lamps, a drawer full of bent forks and blunt butter knives but never enough spoons. The bedding, however worn, always smelled fresh. And of course, there was the outdoor privy.

Depending on the conviviality of the group, medium- and large-size cabins could hold from four to ten people. The most important limiting factor as to the number of occupants was the size of bucket in the outhouse adjacent to each cabin. "Buckets," as the boy or girl who cleaned the outhouses was known, only made one pickup per day.

The main attraction was the lodge itself. The owner and proprietor for the first 25 years until his death in the 1950s was Jack Nelson. His wife Tressa cooked and cleaned. His sister Ruby ramrodded the remote resort business. Thousands of Northwesterners sought out the legendary Sunday evening lodge dinners prepared by Tressa and Ruby.

Getting to Harmony Falls Lodge meant getting away from everything else, literally. In 1931, the road to Spirit Lake was wide enough for one car. If you met an oncoming car, one of you had to back up to a wide place in the road.

The bridges that withstood the annual flood of snowmelt were rickety. Never mind the bridges, though. Most times tourists back then simply barrelled their jalopies across milkshake rivers brimming with pinkish volcanic ash and glacial flour washed down the snowy flanks of Mount St. Helens.

Jack, Tressa and Ruby lived in the lodge. Guests stayed in the cabins. Some cabin guests cooked their own meals. Others joined the Nelsons for their homestyled fixings. College kids were often recruited from the summer camps to work the following summers as kitchen girls. They would stay all summer, from Memorial Day to Labor Day.

Kitchen help was always needed during the busy summertime. In 1945, the pay was $3.50 a day, plus tips, room and board. Duties included peeling potatoes, slicing carrots and serving meals. Ruby sternly admonished the help to braid their hair and wear white anklets, since during World War II it was impossible to get protective hairnets and rayon stockings.

"To get up into our room, we climbed a ladder where stood two cots and two orange crates, each with a kerosene lamp on top. I learned immediately never to remove the glass lantern after the flame had been burning all evening," recalled Patty Otis Dyke of her "kitchen help" days at the end of World War II.

The place was in constant disrepair, usually from winter storm damage. But that's the way Harmony Falls was. That was the fun-ness of the place. Something was always falling down.

Since there was little light inside the cabins, the best place to hang a mirror was on an outside wall. None of the mirrors were very good. Faces appeared lopsided or cracked.

There were no shower stalls or bathtubs, only small, granite gray washbasins in which young girls shampooed their hair, old men soaked their feet and chatterbox children took their baths. The furniture was wonderfully creaky and so were the beds. But never mind the miserable conditions. That was part of the Harmony Falls experience.

41

Jack and Tressa stayed year round at the lodge. Guests hiked and boated to the lodge in the summer and tramped in wearing snowshoes after Christmas. Tressa was a big, quiet woman with sparkly brown eyes and an always welcoming smile. She cooked with a dignified confidence that knew exactly how brown the pie crust should be. Her secret was a dab of bacon grease added to the pie dough. She smelled like warm bread. Her hands were floury. On the waterfront or hiking a trail through the backcountry, she appeared lost. Her domain was the kitchen, concocting brown-sugared carrots or floating an onion peel for flavor in her Red French Dressing.

Harmony Falls' refrigerator was the icy waterfalls behind the lodge. The kitchen help scurried back and forth between the lodge and the falls. They pulled back the wet gunnysacks that covered the great crocks wedged between logs and rocks. The ceramic crocks were crammed with raw chickens, thick pink steaks, raw milk, heavy cream, crisp lettuce, pounds and pounds of butter and fresh brown eggs. Before they could fill their boxes with meat or pitchers with cream, the staffers drenched themselves in the mist of the falls, a condition which few minded on hot summer days.

Ruby was tough. She handled kitchen duties, supervised the help, collected rents and ran the business. She could be a stern taskmaster when necessary. The Nelsons' nephew, Boyd, and another boy, Ray Packwood, hauled drinking water from the lake or stream for the lodgers' first night. Thus could Ruby boast of her "running water."

Boyd's main chores besides splitting wood for heating and cooking included dumping the filled cans from each cabin's "dooley" and replacing them with fresh cans containing several inches of clean water whitened with Hexol. Young Ray's chores consisted of wheelbarrowing suitcases from the *Tressa* or the *Ruby* to the cabins. When urged to do so, he recited "Abou Ben Ahdem."

The staff never ate dinner until dishes were done and they rarely ate chicken or steak. Their fare consisted of shortribs, fried ham, potatoes, applesauce and pork, garden green beans, peas, and pans of blueberry or cherry cobbler. Sometimes Tressa whipped up her special bread pudding flavored with plump raisins and topped with nutmeg. And cream, lots of thick, rich cream on top of everything. The help seldom lost weight during their summer stays at Harmony Falls.

Ruby's brother Jack had the strength to muscle the green rowboats out of the water for recaulking and repairs. Chores never stopped, nor did Nelson's kindly demeanor. He could swing the hammer when need be. Early in the morning, he might chop an emergency armload of kindling for his guests and gladly take in exchange his "morning's morning," a coffee mug of bourbon.

The Schauffler family cabin was typical of those at Harmony Falls. With three rooms and a vaulted ceiling supported by thick eaves, it was perfect for kids jumping on just-made beds. The Schauffler family preferred their own cabin with its big, round table for dinners and cards, reserving meals at the main lodge for special occasions.

Inside the Schauffler's cabin was a stove for cooking and baking and some shelves between the bare stud framing for books. And of course there was the great, shaggy drape. The long misused drape divided the bedroom and doubled as a Tarzan vine and theater curtain for melodramatic performances by the family's budding thespians.

After guests had departed the Schauffler cabin, Tressa and the help liked to row over from the main lodge in one of the flat bottom boats to a log with cleated steps nailed on it. After tying up to the base of the log, the three women would scamper up the log slanting up the bank with clean linens, brooms, towels and mops. The routine included airing out the cast-iron Hudson Bay blankets and splashing down the floors with buckets of clear lake water before the final sweeping. The routine was much the same for the other cabins, except for the honeymooners' lodge. It was swept sweet and clean with water dipped directly from Harmony Falls.

Julia Schauffler Bernard recalled that from her first trip to the lake in 1931 at the age of three or four, Portland families united year after year at Harmony Falls. Many owned their cabins, which Jack Nelson leased out during the short summer tourist season. She remembered lots of Schaufflers, Koehlers and Malarkeys, and dozens of others from Portland, Longview, all over.

And there was Old Bill, the sourdough logger, in his same old leather pants with suspenders. He split many a round of wood for cabin dwellers there at Harmony.

People came and went through the years, and their numbers gradually increased with the improvements to the Spirit Lake Highway in the late 1930s.

"But of all the places that I have been and know, I think it changed less than any other place I've been. One of the reasons, I think, is that the road came in and more or less stopped right there. It did not go all the way around the lake to Harmony Falls," Bernard said.

Campfires brought the lodgers together after days spent hiking and swimming, sailing and huckleberry picking. Even in the rain! One of Bernard's favorite memories was of the storyteller Wayne Coe, son of Portlander Dr. Henry Coe. A large figure in a great slouch hat and a tarpaulin pulled over his shoulders, he strode down the slippery cant steps and crossed the grounds to the campfire where he stood motionless, dripping wet. His long, soft eyelids drooped over a pair of deep blue eyes. Rain crackled in the fir boughs above the cabins.

"Forty years, man and boy, and I've never seen it rain at Spirit Lake," he said.

The kids roared, "Oh haaah!" Their parents grimaced in mock pain.

He summoned a deep breath and launched into the saying once again: "Forty years, man and..."

"Oh haaah!" the kids yelled again, interrupting him this time.

When it rained at Spirit Lake, everything got wet, really wet. A person has never been so wet as the wet he or she could get when it rained at Spirit Lake. "Forty years, man and boy, and I've never seen it rain at Spirit Lake." For years the famous saying warded off the effects of the frequent rain showers at Harmony Falls.

In the summer of 1943, there was music on the porch of the Gov'ners Mansion. Dr. Goodrich Schauffler cocked the violin under his chin and focused hard on the back and forth motion of his bow. Wilma Muhlenberg swayed to the left and then the right to the rhythm of the wilderness while Nick Muhlenberg held his own on the violin by her side. The warm glow of the setting sun shined in the faces of Allen Schauffler, Jack Healy, Tom Malarkey and Bob Brown before it disappeared into the pointy tops of 300-year-old Douglas firs on a distant mountain range.

A chilly, rainy evening in Harmony brought a person in tune with friends and relatives. You sipped hot cocoa from thick, heavy cups. You pondered the music of the rain beating against the cedar shakes. You sucked the skin off huckleberries and squished the sweet pulp with your tongue against the top of your mouth. You leaned into a warm shadow in the cabin corner across from the wood stove. You listened to a ghost story about the hairy apes of Mount St. Helens. You laughed about the mythical submarine believed to lurk beneath the waves of Spirit Lake. Then it was bedtime.

* * *

The Longview YMCA Camp neighbored Harmony Falls Lodge. The counselors and staff at the camp were amiable towards the Nelsons and always appreciative of an occasional slice of huckleberry pie or a boat ride.

When the last of the campers had departed the Longview "Y" camp in mid-August, the counselors spent a week or two closing up for winter. Windows were shuttered, walls and roofs braced for snow loading and water pipes drained. Benches were stacked and boats beached. Autumn mists were already issuing stern warnings of early winter snowfalls. It was during this time that the "Y" camp counselors were most vulnerable to the taunts of the

Harmony Falls crowd to desert their duties and compete in water sports.

Dozens of "looker-on'ers" crowded the logs along the banks for a clear view of the canoe races. Log-rolling and boat-pulling brought cheers from the makeshift bleachers. Spirits soared. The hoots and cheers would be the last heard in such volume before the end of yet another year. For the participants, the experience was a rite of passage, from boyhood to manhood, girlhood to womanhood. This was competition at its keenest, one last dip in the ice water of Spirit Lake.

Swimming in Spirit Lake required a suspension of good sense. The cold tightened the muscles and purged the body of wimpy afflictions. The ice water down below made the unstable diving platform all the more terrifying. Two kids or one medium sized adult standing on the end of the board caused it to lean and gradually sink to the right until the whole thing submerged. Burial at sea, especially in the Harmony Falls swimming area, was never a pretty sight, but it encouraged boisterous laughter.

Incredible, unnatural phenomena were commonplace. Like the time a big man with a balding pate climbed the diving platform puffing away on a big cigar. Kids stopped and stared as the man dived off the board, which was incredible in itself. But then to surface with the cigar still lighted was bizarre. Such became the stuff of many a kid's "What I Did Last Summer" essay.

The lake was a little more than a mile across. The distance challenged Spirit Lake people at Harmony Falls every year. The brave and the foolish slickered up with bacon grease and swam across when they felt particularly daring. The accomplishment for many is a memory that can never be duplicated.

The premier lake contest was The Regatta. This was the contest of wits, skill, strength and cunning. The winner would be the young man best able to pilot his sleek sailboat amidst the cat's paw wavelets kicked up by the changeable winds on Spirit Lake. Mssrs. Henry Cabell and Aubrey Morgan officiated at the gala event, ever the diplomats, ever fair-minded, for this event, however insignificant in terms of world events was of utmost importance to 18-year-old boys testing themselves against the elements and each other.

Afternoons and evenings at Harmony were consumed with dramatic performances, poetry contests, art shows and hat parties. Wine and cheese for adults, lemonade for the little guys, preceded the usual parade at one of "Aunt Deedlie's" parties, presided over by a distinguished panel of dads. As the mood possessed the group, the competition would shift from freeform hat design to freeform sculpture. A skinned banana on a cracked plate, entitled "Of Banana," stole all the honors one year. Another year a great half of a bandsaw blade, fabricated to a rusty roundsaw blade, made for the gong show award winner.

After dinner in the various cabins, the families converged on the lodge for bag skits or mountain music. When the group arrived, they were divided into six or eight teams of players, each with a bag of props. They each made up a play to go with the props, then spent the rest of the evening taking turns performing. They also danced to homegrown music made on guitars and banjos, a folding organ, recorders and flutes, or the violin. The rhythm and beat changed with the times. No one could ever explain how Jack Nelson got that piano across the lake to the lodge.

Alice Malarkey Koehler recalled her teenage years at Harmony Falls for the good times made by the kids themselves. "We used to play a marvelous game called Up Jenkins with a quarter. You passed the quarter underneath the table. The other team asked us to do three different things like 'Do an elephant walk,' or 'Do creepy crawly.' You were supposed to hear the quarter go clink. Then they had to guess where the quarter was. For some reason, it got very raucous. That was a good game."

Koehler's father and mother began vacationing at Spirit Lake with the Schauffler family in 1929. In the early 1950s, Neil Malarkey and his brother-in-law, John W.S. Platt, bought Harmony Falls Lodge for $10,000 from Wayne Coe. Many of the families that comprised the 10-day, live-in commune every August bought shares from the Malarkeys and Platts in what became Harmony Falls Corporation. Cost of the shares was based on the value of the timber. The purpose of their investment was to preserve the ambience of the little Spirit Lake community that had come to mean so much to their families.

"We always wanted it run as a public resort because the health of Harmony Falls depended on people filling up those cabins and using it. Even as owners when we went there for a week we paid because we leased the place out. Otherwise there would have been ten days without revenue. The season was usually the middle of June until the end of September. We usually went the end of August.

"It always rained the end of August. We picked that time because, if children had jobs, they could always quit their jobs. It was really very family-oriented. Everybody wanted to be there.

"When we were teenagers, my father organized the Spirit Lake Olympics. We had one day of racing and running and a treasure hunt. Everybody participated. That was about 50 or 60 people because we all had big families. When we would go up for our time, we saw to it that all the cabins were rented. They were all our friends. We took over the whole place for a week or 10 days," recalled Koehler.

46

Though there was some organization at Harmony Falls, especially around mealtime, most of the activity was spontaneous.

World events, even regional politics, could not compete for table debate with the often-discussed rumors of an early snowstorm, a tragic drowning or the temper of a black bear.

Nelson himself was one of the main attractions. Guests talked about him, the size of his huge hands, the kindness he showed a child, his feats of strength, his stories of the hairy apes who inhabited the south side of the mountain. At the center of the ever constant speculation about Jack Nelson was his fabled relationship with Harry Truman, owner and proprietor of Mount St. Helens Lodge on the southwestern side of the lake.

Nelson and Truman could not have been less alike. Jack Nelson was the amiable, likeable, self-educated Indianan, a philosopher, who could discuss the plot in John Steinbeck's *The Red Pony,* but was just as anxious to share a drink with a guest behind the woodlot. Harry Truman was mean-spirited, irascible and unpredictable. A proud West Virginian, Truman drank a bit, too. Together, on the same lake, oftentimes dependent on each other if there was a problem in the remote Spirit Lake area, Nelson and Truman were unlikely neighbors, but made great topics of conversation among Spirit Lake people.

The story goes that Truman originally sought out the seclusion of Spirit Lake in 1926 after hearing that gangsters he had crossed in California were in hot pursuit. He and his first wife Helen hurriedly abandoned his Harry's Sudden Service gas station in Chehalis, Washington, and split for Spirit Lake. There, he shared a gas station and log cabin grocery on the south side of the lake with Nelson.

The two squabbled over the rental boats and grimaced at how each treated the customers. Nelson was too accommodating. Truman, too intolerant. They shook their heads when confronting the future. In 1928 they parted company. Nelson sold out to Truman and then moved two miles to the farthest corner of the lake to build his Harmony Falls Lodge.

"He and Truman were deadly enemies. They hated each other and never went out of their way to do anything for each other. Jack Nelson couldn't swim and here he owned a resort on a lake. Truman saved his life one time early on because he was drowning. I don't know what happened to them but they really never spoke to each other," recalled Mrs. Koehler.

The rift between Truman and Nelson was noticed by a couple of newcomers to Harmony Falls one hot July in 1950. They were John W.S. Platt and his wife Jane Kerr Platt.

"When we first started going up to Harmony Falls, I don't think Jack

Nelson and Harry Truman got along all that well. They were competitors and they were both sort of characters," said Platt.

"Most of the people who used to stay at Harmony Falls with the Nelsons came under the influence of their opinion. The word was spread that Harry Truman was a very difficult guy. He had these speedboats, runabout type boats made of mahogany, beautiful boats. He used to charge people and take them sightseeing around the lake at a pretty fast clip and would send up these big waves. Well, that used to annoy everyone down at that end of the lake, so they were prepared to think Harry Truman was sort of a pain in the neck."

But Platt himself said, "I had a very high regard for Harry."

It is true, agreed Platt, that Truman did not have very many good friends, but there was a reason: "I don't think very many people earned the privilege."

Platt originally came to Harmony Falls at the invitation of his sister, Sue who with her husband Neil Malarkey were cabin owners and veteran summertime residents of the hideaway. Platt recalled one weekend in July:

"We thoroughly enjoyed it, so the following year, we went up with our oldest son, John, who was then about eight. Then, the year after that, we rented one of the cabins and were able to take our youngest son, David, who was then about four."

During their forays to Spirit Lake, the Platts noticed a particularly beautiful cabin on the north end of the lake near the YMCA camp. It seemed abandoned. Platt inquired and determined that former YMCA camp director and founder, John C. Meehan and his wife once lived there before his death a few years earlier.

"It was a remarkable little cabin, extremely well built to withstand very heavy snowfalls. We made the YMCA an offer, which seemed like a lot of money at the time. My recolletion is that it was $9,000."

The Portland YMCA accepted the offer with the option of buying back the cabin in 10 years for the same price plus the appreciated value of the improvements.

"There wasn't much deeded land on that lake. And, in fact, ours was the only private cabin on deeded land up there," Platt said.

The cabin itself was merely a place, like the cabins that dotted the various summer camps or sprouted up around Harmony Falls Lodge and Mount St. Helens Lodge. A dwelling, after all, is but a roof and four walls. What happened to the spirits of the Platt family made the cabin unique, though. Platt recalled the spring of 1954:

"As soon as the snow cleared off the lake, I went up there by myself to open the cabin. I remember waking up the first morning early and going down on the dock. I had my fishing rod with me and cast out into the lake. On the second cast, I got a fish. Spirit Lake had never been noted for its fishing—most of the fish were planted—but this was a very respectable trout. So I cast out again and got another fish. When I was unhooking that second fish, I heard a splash or something—a commotion—and I turned and here was a family of otters coming up to the edge of the lake and playing and fishing and having a marvelous time.

"I remember thinking, can this be possible? Am I here? Is this ours? To me, it just seemed like some form of heaven. I remember the feeling so clearly and vividly and, of course, I was the only one up there. You could hear forever under those conditions."

The Platts were part-time residents only a short while when Jack Nelson, the able proprietor of Harmony Falls Lodge, died. His passing shocked and saddened the Harmony Falls community. Tressa and Ruby carried on, but the storytelling Nelson was impossible to replace. Harmony Falls would never be quite the same. Harry Truman's nemesis was dead.

Friends of the Nelsons pitched in with the lodge management. Tressa and Ruby hired on summer help, too. After a few years, though, it became obvious to Neil Malarkey and John Platt that Tressa and Ruby were being overwhelmed without Jack because of increasing crowds of tourists.

Thus did Harmony Falls as a company come into existence. At first, it was the Malarkeys, then came to include the Platts, then gradually other families pitched in to retain the precious quality that they had enjoyed since the 1930s. But times had changed, vastly.

Platt recalled those troubled days and the succession of managers after Tressa and Ruby left. None could replace the Nelsons. Harmony Falls cried out for leadership. Instead, what it got in the 1960s and early 1970s was a series of managers who, despite the best of intentions, failed to measure up to the Nelsons' tireless spirit, their sensible volubility, their unselfish devotion to their lodgers and others who loved Spirit Lake as much as they did. Some of the managers regarded Harmony Falls as their private reserve, and that prompted the eight or so families of Harmony Falls Corporation to actively seek out a better management team.

"Well, that wasn't what we had in mind and the place was going downhill, very decidedly. It was at that point that we then got ahold of the Berrys—Laurie and David. It was a very fortunate happening for everyone," Platt said.

The daughter of Julia Schauffler Bernard, Laura Berry was perfect because she recalled her own childhood meals prepared at Harmony Falls Lodge by Tressa Nelson. She remembered the taste of Tressa's steak and milk gravy, boiled potatoes and candied carrots, her hot bread and heavy cream, chicken dinners and huckleberry pie. Under the Berrys' management of the resort, the old Harmony Falls habitues returned in droves.

"Everyone was terribly pleased that this had occurred. They were a young couple but they were just doing a marvelous job and Harmony Falls was really coming back. It was sold out a year in advance and we were all terribly encouraged," said Platt.

For six years, the Berrys mailed calligraphic letters to Northwesterners who vacationed at the lodge, announcing the menu, the cabin rates and the activities. Nothing new, mind you. Just hiking. Backpacking. Mountain climbing. Fishing. Singing. Playing. Competing. And there was still the regatta during that magic week in August that had become known to many as "Malarkey Week."

The resort with its 10 cabins remained open to one and all during the short summer season and was experiencing a renaissance until May 18, 1980, the day Mount St. Helens obliterated Harmony Falls.

"We've tried to think of other places where the Berrys could go and run a lodge because they did it so well and were so well suited to it," said Platt.

Alas, Harmony Falls as a gathering spot was irreplaceable. The spirit of the people who collected there for 50 years, however, is inextinguishable.

Chapter VII

Keeping up With the Joneses

Ambition drove Jake Jones into the windless, snowy forest, dark as a wolf's mouth, along the treacherous North Fork of the winding Toutle River. Head down, the 28-year-old man mushed his cross-country skis through the snow.

Up ahead of Jake, his brother, Alden, 31, set a vicious pace, poling into the snow with the determination of a linebacker. Let's get this over with! Behind Jake, his other brother, Clark, 24, pounded out a grunting sound as though he were singing under his breath. Maybe he was. Bringing up the rear was Howard McCorkle, a family friend of the Jones boys. Like Jake, Howard was also 28 years old.

Howard was better at cranking his elbow at the local tavern back home in Kelso than he was at mountain climbing. But what the heck, he rated! After all, anybody foolhardy enough to keep up with the Joneses this far deserved the chance to scale Mount St. Helens the first few hours of January 1, 1938.

New Year's Day on Mount St. Helens began warmly enough a few hours earlier at the Elk Creek ranger station with a bracing cup of tea and some sandwiches. Now it was 5 a.m. The four men skied over crusted snow through the tunnel of fir, cedar, hemlock, and some bent over alder. Downed trees

51

broke their stride, forcing them to sidestep this way, then that.

Not a word was said though as the foursome pressed onward in a relentless race against a cold winter sun not yet on the horizon. One-half mile west of Spirit Lake Lodge, Alden steered southward off the road into Dry Gulch.

Suddenly, as only the sun can do in alpine country, there was light, pure, clear, piercing and radiant. Out came the dense sunglasses. Alden leaned into his poles. Now the climb would begin. Let's get this over with!

Jake had first climbed St. Helens 10 years earlier. He and Allen Dibble— 18-year-old fools. They risked their necks one hot August day in 1928. Since then, Jake had climbed the mountain more than 50 times.

His feats were not without risks, even after he learned better how to assault the lofty peak. For instance, there was that time a few years earlier, back in the winter of 1930, when he slipped just below the Dogs Head. He was climbing without crampons. He was not roped to his partners. And now, he could not stop. For a thousand feet he slid. He finally piled up on an island of rocks, his elbow bloody and permanently scarred.

Jake developed great expertise at scaling St. Helens and was often called on to lead climbs by the YMCA and the Longview Hiking Club. Indeed, he was so accustomed to the moods of the mountain that he resorted to pranks to give his climbs more vitality. Like the time in 1934 when he sneaked up the mountain in the middle of the night and "planted" a watermelon. The next day when the Hiking Club arrived at the summit, Jake said, "Just a minute, I think I'll go and see how my watermelon patch is." He went over to the ridge and brought back this ice cold melon for the crew to feast on.

Today would be different, though. Today Jake was climbing with his brothers on the very first day of the New Year. This would be a day to remember.

The four men huffed down Dry Gulch and then gradually upwards as the slopes tilted skyward.

Clark barked, "It's already nine o'clock. We should've started sooner."

Jake tapped his jacket pocket inside his coat. If today was rough, he would be calling on the instant energy of the little honey bottle he kept thawed close to his own body.

Howard was panting as the trees shrank from view into the snow far down below. In this country, the usually majestic fir bends over in gnarled obedience, her limbs withered from winter's onslaught. At 10 o'clock, Alden looked over his shoulder and gave the command to hold up by a small fir tree.

"Thank God," panted Howard. He dropped in his tracks, then quickly regained his balance and composure. Nine miles they had hiked.

Jake rummaged around in his pack, which was carefully strapped to an alder wood packboard. He pulled out his thermos. Some hot vegetable soup now might spell the difference later between surviving a fall into a crevasse, or dying.

"I wonder if Sam's up yet," Clark asked the group. They stared down through the timberline to the curved open area that was Spirit Lake. Smoke from a warming fire — or was it some wind-whipped snow clouds? — blew off the treetops beside the snow-covered surface of the lake. If one of the climbers took a spill today, "Sam" Samuelson, the resident ranger for the U.S. Forest Service, would be the "help" the boys would have to go for. Other than the smoke, there was no sign of life at any of the lodges sprinkled around the banks of Spirit Lake.

Alden unstrapped his skis and planted them beside the fir. Clark and Howard did the same, followed by Jake.

The soft powdery snow at first made traveling hard, but it soon gave way to a crust. Their steps held. The moon was long gone. Clear. Cold. Goat Rocks beckoned from the 6,000-foot level far above them. The four trekked eastwardly around St. Helens towards the Sugar Bowl.

The climb at this stage seemed easy enough. The sun arched skyward around the smooth shoulder of the mountain but then a stiff wind kicked up from the southwest as the four reached the lower part of the Big Lizard.

"You know, Babe Ruth can slug 'em, but I'd trade him for a Lige Coalman on a day like today," Jake said of one of the better-known mountain men who was legend to outdoorsmen between Mount Rainier and Mount Hood."

"Yeah, I know what you mean. I'm feeling it today, too," said Al.

"Me too," said a slightly worried rearguard. Poor Howard was not looking so good.

Clark shook his head a bit and kept quiet. He rocked back and contemplated the view of the hulking Mount Rainier far to the north, shrouded as it usually is in its own veil of weather. Even Lige Coalman would be huffing and puffing up this mountain today! Let's get on with it!

Alden slipped his packboard from his back and reached into the bag for his heaviest wool sweater. He had to disrobe and then bundle up again quickly lest he lose the precious body heat vital to survival in these arctic conditions. The wind almost ripped the sweater from his grip.

Howard and Clark did the same. They would all need every stitch of clothing they had thought to bring today. Was it 20 below? With each wave of wind crashing over the landscape the temperature seemed to drop 10 degrees. What did it matter after the freezing mark was shattered?

Jake unwrapped a block of Hershey's chocolate. He already had on his extra sweater. Like the others, his total attire was two wool shirts, two sweaters, wool underwear, gabardine ski pants, ski shoes, two pairs of socks, a wool scarf, two pairs of mittens, a wool cap and that trusty, but un-water-proofed, parka. And crampons. Many a time he had crawled off a glacier or out from the gaping mouth of a crevasse with those boogers.

"Alden, my fingers are really numb," said Clark, finally breaking his silence. It had been obvious though, the way he had been rubbing and clapping his heavily-clad hands together the past five minutes.

"Here, put them inside my parka," said Jake to his brother.

Howard's hands were freezing too, as were Alden's. So they carefully inserted their hands inside each other's parka, under each other's armpits. Howard grimaced. Similarly, Alden winced in pain as the circulation returned to his frozen limbs.

Jake's circulation was just fine, in fact, great. He prided himself on his health, his utter fitness from working in the Northwest woods. He had spent 1937 drawing contour maps for Weyerhaeuser from the solitude of the tall timber all around Mount St. Helens. He also had run transit for Al, who likewise worked in the cartography section for Weyerhaeuser. What he thrived on though was the outdoors and the long life he swore it would bring to those who earned their living in the woods. Office work kills a man 20 years before his time, according to Jake's way of thinking.

"All right, let's get going," said Alden, ever in command. Only now he deferred to Jake's leadership at chopping steps into the snow. The driving wind dumped snow and sleet on the four. Jake dug a step, then two, into the crusty snowcover. Then from his perch on the two new steps he would drive the open face of his ice axe deep into the Lizard. The Boot loomed off to Jake's right, The Island to his left. He reckoned they were at the 8,500-foot level, another thousand feet to go.

"Take over Al," he said, sinking into his footsteps a second longer than he should have. Exhaustion pile-drived down on him. He reached for his jar of honey and sucked hard on it for that extra rush of energy.

Clark swigged hot tea from his thermos, then passed it to Howard who took an equally long drag. The hot fluid scalded the inside of his mouth, the sweetness of the tea instantly radiating out through his chest and stomach and somehow warming his toes.

Jake took one more suck on his honey jar and leapfrogged around Alden who was six steps ahead of the climbers by now.

"Here, I'll chop a few now," said Jake. Together, he and Al worked their way ahead, advancing the group 10 yards at a time.

Each climber attempted minor improvements to the staircase. Clark was swinging furiously on one particular step when the tip of his ice axe caught his wrist between his mitten and his parka. The icy cold steel electrified him. His body shivered. No mark would be found later on his hand, but the cold metal made its mark on his memory for life.

Gritty snow and ice flecks tore into their eyelids and encrusted the exposed hair on their foreheads, their eyebrows and even the few exposed hairs inside their nostrils. Jake thought his nose was freezing solid. He pulled his hand from his mitten and squeezed the tip of his nose. It cracked down and stayed down until he inserted his fingers into his nostrils and opened the holes again.

Al pulled out a concrete chocolate bar, chawed off a chunk, then passed it back to Jake. He did the same and passed it to Clark and from him to Howard. This ritual was understood. The stuff of life. Nothing needed to be said amidst the wind howling down on the mortals like an angry banshee.

"Hey Al, do ya' think we ought'a rope up?" asked a plaintive Howard. He appeared lost. A rope means direction, a pathway to follow, life. Al thought yes but a quick check with Jake changed his mind. No, no, no, Jake was shaking his head.

"By the time we get laced together we may as well all jump into Forsyth Glacier for the slow ride down next century. We'd all freeze tryin' to tie on. Let's just keep going and get this over with," Jake said.

"Just use your ice axe, Howard, and dig in with your crampons," said Alden.

"Yeah, that is if you can still feel your toes. I can't even feel my feet anymore," said Howard. Clark looked at him and nodded his head. Jake suddenly realized that Clark was suffering the effects of cold, too, only it was like him to not say a word. Let's get this over with!

The sky was still bright and sunny, deceptively sunny. Off in the distance, black storm clouds roiled out of a hole in the horizon, obscuring Mount Rainier and then Mount Adams. The wind plastered the four climbers to the north face of St. Helens.

"I'm not so sure . . ." Howard started out but his voice was muffled by the icy hand of the wind.

The steps were absolutely required now to surmount The Boot at the 9,000-foot level. Jake surveyed the situation. His older brother Al was fading a bit in the stretch, as was Howard. Clark was mum, but that was characteristic. If Clark was frostbitten from his knees down he would not mention it until the hike was history. That was his way.

"We can make it boys, just don't stop at False Summit," said Jake, determined as ever to be the first to conquer Mount St. Helens in 1938.

The danger, as Jake saw it, was not in the threat to one's toes or fingers from frostbite. Nor was he afraid of hypothermia. No, what Jake was most concerned about was turning around too soon because of the deceptive topography of Mount St. Helens' volcanic cone. He was fearful that his fatigued crew might mistake the lower rim of that cone for the genuine summit, which it emphatically was not. No way would Jake let them not finish the last 100 feet to the true rim at 9,677 feet.

Finally, at 3:15 p.m., January 1, 1938, the four braced themselves against the wind, gusting to 50 miles per hour as they reached the summit.

"Wanta' race for the look-out," Jake challenged the others. The old Forest Service fire watch station, erected 20 years earlier and abandoned 10 years later in 1928, required too much energy, even for a quick scamper. Alden and Howard shook their heads and Clark turned to descend after taking two quick snapshots of the victors and their snowy, windswept conquest.

The trip down was incredibly fast. One hour and 10 minutes later they were at timberline once again. Howard slipped a can of tomato juice from his pack. It was frozen, but they all chipped at it anyway. Clark's feet were awful. Three toes appeared frost-bitten. The climb had taken its toll.

Jake soaked in the scene. His two brothers and a friend, alive, atop the world with Spirit Lake far down below. Now it was 1938. Time to start a New Year. Time for the boys to find wives. Time to settle down to family life. Time to sketch contours for Weyerhaeuser and stay fit, grow old, cherish friends, nourish families and love life. That's all there is. Muscle, guts and luck.

Images

Robert and Minnie Lange at their Spirit Lake homestead,
c. 1923

Charles Thomas, husband-to-be of Lillian Lange, with wagon team on timberline road construction project headed up by Grandpa Lange,
c. 1914

Georgia (left) and Julia Lange in their Sunday best in front of the second Lange homestead one Sunday day,
c. Spring, 1915

Robert Lange (left) with an unidentified miner (center) and Lange's son, William, take a break on the bunkhouse steps. The kitchen building is at the left rear and the mill powerhouse is in the center of the three buildings, c. 1912

Minnie Lange in the doorway of the family's first cabin at Spirit Lake, c. 1900

John C. Meehan and his charges at the Portland YMCA's Camp Blister on the south side of Spirit Lake, c. 1912

"1-2-3 GO!"
c. 1913

"Y" campers loading their gear into Mr. Burnside's wagon for the grueling three-day trip to Spirit Lake. While their bags rode, the boys walked.
c. 1913

Boys headed for summer camp at Spirit Lake board an open lorry parked in front of the Portland YMCA, c. 1924

Passengers and crew aboard the 127-foot sternwheeler Joseph Kellogg hold up a moment before launching on an excursion up the Cowlitz River to Kelso, Washington—the jump-off point for Mount St. Helens!
c. 1881

Jaunty climbers pose in front of the Forest Service's lookout on the summit of Mount St. Helens at a time when George Schnitgler manned the remote fire watchtower. Built in 1916 and placed in service in 1917, the lookout was abandoned 10 years later in favor of lower elevation sites.
c. September 1, 1924

Dark sunglasses were an obvious necessity for these climbers shortly after sunrise somewhere on the western slope of Mount St. Helens.
c. July, 1928

After weeks of "fitness" hikes, these YMCA campers scaled the pinnacle with little more in the way of mountaineering gear than the alpenstocks crafted from broom handles. Note the tin cups hitched to their belts. Lipstick and facial creams were applied for skin protection.
c. July 1928

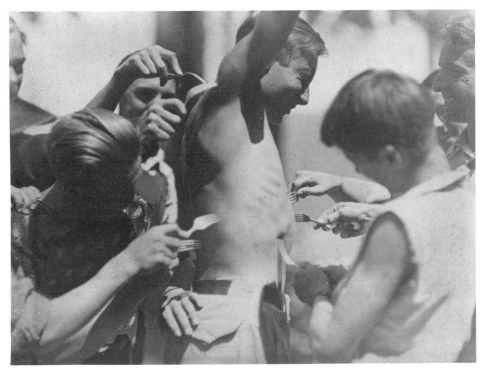

The four-pronged initiation to the Spirit Lake "forker's club" tested the nerve of many a boy attending the Spirit Lake "Y" camp.
c. 1924

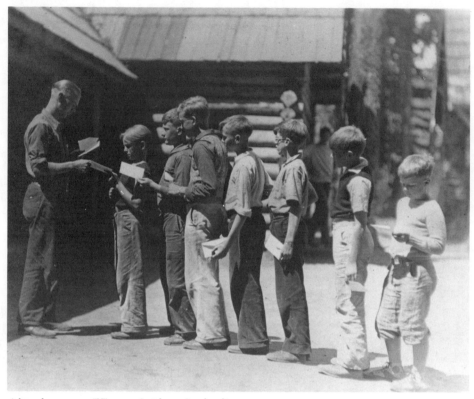

A letter home was a "Y" camper's ticket to Sunday dinner.
c. 1924

Legendary mountaineer Lige Coalman inspired hundreds of boys during the years he helped manage the Portland "Y" camp at Spirit Lake between 1926 and 1937. This photo was taken during a break in construction of Holmstedt Memorial Lodge, which Coalman built with Fred Bradley of the Forest Service and a pioneer named Louis Umiker.
c. Fall, 1927

Ape Canyon as seen through the camera lens of amateur botanist and photographer Gunnar Nilsson. Snow-capped Mount Adams looms on the horizon to the east.
c. 1950

Forest Service Ranger Harold "Sam" Samuelson muses a moment on the store steps at Spirit Lake. The tall, slim "Ranger of Spirit Lake" from the 1920s until his retirement in 1958, employed quiet diplomacy to maintain order in the Gifford Pinchot National Forest. c. Early 1940s

Weyerhaeuser logging boss Russell Carmichael (closest to the end of log) lines up his logging crew for a picture to memorialize this record old-growth Douglas fir felled near Mount St. Helens.
c. July 26, 1944

At the helm of the Tressa *half way across Spirit Lake, Harmony Falls Lodge proprietor Jack Nelson gazes quizzically into the camera lens of Gunnar Nilsson, his longtime friend and occasional guest. c. 1938*

Neskowin photographer Goodwin Harding captured the essence of Harmony Falls Lodge in this inviting shot taken from the Spirit Lake waterfront.
c. 1979

Dr. Goodrich Schauffler on violin, Wilma Muhlenberg on organ, and her son Nick also on violin, provide onlookers with cocktail hour music on the porch of the Gov'nor's Mansion at Harmony Falls Lodge while the sun settles in the west. Looking on (from the left) are Allen Schauffler, Jack Healy, Tom Malarkey and Bob Brown (seated).
c. 1943

Harry Truman with his famed boats for rent,
c. 1953

Spirit Lake Lodge shortly after opening for the tourist season,
c. Summer, 1938.

Campers wave from log fence at Camp Meehan,
c. 1943

Ole's Cave
c. Late 1940s

St. Helens hermit Ole Peterson lights his pipe.
c. Late 1940s

Ole Peterson
c. Late 1940s

Ole Peterson's cabin near Swift Creek on south side of Mount St. Helens,
c. Late 1940s

Gunnar Nilsson reconnoiters seracs near the summit of St. Helens.
c. Late 1930s

Longview Ski Club members unload from the "cat" and ready themselves for the descent to their club lodge at the timberline of Mount St. Helens.
c. Late 1940s

Chapter VIII

Fire Watch at Spirit Lake

Today, Jim Langdon might be regarded as a sexist porker. But back in 1941, he was pretty liberated. At least compared to other forest rangers, he was openminded. It was this quality that probably resulted in the prevention of a few forest fires while simultaneously offering a handful of women some bold opportunities previously unavailable to women here in the Northwest.

Langdon had been the Spirit Lake ranger and superintendent of the Civilian Conservation Corps for five years when the Japanese bombed Pearl Harbor, December 7, 1941. The news startled America. Like people everywhere, Langdon began thinking about how the war effort would change his life, his world.

His world was the U.S. Forest Service. Born in the Sellwood district of Portland, Langdon studied landscape architecture at Oregon State University. He started his career in Yellowstone where he worked on Civilian Conservation Corps projects for the Forest Service. He accepted transfers to projects throughout the Northwest before taking his Spirit Lake assignment.

In fall, 1935, Langdon gazed upon the creamy symmetry of St. Helens from the north side of Spirit Lake and knew that this peak stood apart from all the other snowcapped giants that made up the Cascade Range.

St. Helens was different. It was a new mountain. There was little erosion. A big dish of ice cream, St. Helens' snow was often wet and heavy, too sticky for skiers who preferred Rainier and Hood.

There was little surface water and a lot of pumice on St. Helens. The transition from the timbered areas around Mounts Rainier, Hood and Adams all feature alpine flower meadows in which deer and elk flourish. The transition on St. Helens from the closed canopy forests that stopped at the tree line was abrupt and a little startling.

Langdon became intimate with St. Helens during his first five years at Spirit Lake. He prided himself on his supervision of the CCC's improvements to the lake area, especially the campground. Now that he sensed war on the horizon, Langdon decided he had better figure out a way to replace all those men who had bucked logs, built road barriers and guarded against forest fires. By far, the most important task was to spot fires and extinguish them before the mountain was damaged.

Langdon decided one way to preserve what he had spent the previous five years building was to enlist couples from local hiking clubs, especially the one in Longview. A husband and wife could spend their vacation in a fire lookout until another couple replaced them two weeks later.

Langdon invited couples interested in fire duty to spend some evenings during the winter months of 1942 in classrooms around Longview learning the craft of fire watching. His fellow rangers taught the future fire watchers to use the big fire finder to pinpoint the source of a distant blaze so they could report it on the fragile land line telephone sets that connected all the towers to Spirit Lake headquarters.

Schoolteacher Hazel Marcellus attended the classes. Her job would end with the school term that spring. Perfect! But when she approached Langdon with the idea, the ranger scowled. No husband? Just yourself? His words even today echoed in her ears: "No, I'm not going to unless I have to."

Spring slipped into summer. A few weeks later, Langdon called to ask Hazel if she would take over Smith Creek Butte Lookout. The last fire watcher —a young man—had quit after a fit of lonesomeness. The lookouts were 10 to 12 miles on foot from Spirit Lake.

"Yes, I'll take it," she replied. Her other choice was to pull green lumber off a moving chain in a mill. Graveyard shift on the greenchain—not much of a choice, she thought, even if the hike to her fire lookout post was a dozen miles, or so.

"I didn't think I was quite greenchain material so I didn't take that."

Hazel was not the only woman sought by Langdon. Helen Leonard had hiked and camped St. Helens since she moved to Longview in 1936. She knew every trail. She asked Ranger "Sam" Samuelson whether the Forest Service would hire single women to fill jobs vacated by men serving overseas.

"I want to put my name in," she told Samuelson. He laughed but told her to write Langdon in Vancouver, Washington. She did. And like Hazel Marcellus, Langdon called Helen for an interview. He asked if she could do map work. She loved map work. Could she do payroll and bookkeeping? No, that was not her strength. He said that would be easy for her to learn. Finally, he acquiesced as he had with Hazel.

"I might as well hire you as any of the men I can get!"

Langdon also hired Mrs. Arnspiker to look after the warehouses, Mrs. Pryor and her two teenage boys for Strawberry Peak Lookout, and Mrs. Rincy and her son and daughter for Mitchell Peak Lookout. Langdon became a laughingstock throughout the Forest Service because of his female staff. By the end of the summer, though, when men were no longer available, the other rangers were starting to call him, wanting to know if any of his women had friends who wanted work.

The women's service at Spirit Lake began shortly after arrival with more woodlore. Hazel learned to split wood. The learning process was about a cord. "There were several girls went up. I guess they thought we'd chop our toes off or something, so the first thing they did was teach us to split wood."

Hazel persisted in her lessons. Her ranger instructor left her in the woods with a compass. She prowled the brush, an eye peeled for bear, sighting through the top of the lens for her bearings until the scenery began to make sense. A trail of breadcrumbs was strictly verboten. She learned her way around.

Langdon monitored the progress of his protegee. Hazel sensed the Forest Service staff were hardly enthusiastic about girls on lookout, but she stayed on through the last week of June. Langdon admired her spirit.

"Then Jim called and wanted me to be lookout the day before the Fourth of July. He said the Muddy River was a favorite fishing spot and everybody from Portland and all around would come up to fish and camp. They were kind of afraid that maybe there would be fires around the Fourth along the Muddy."

A Forest Service packer took Hazel's supplies to the lookout. Her only baggage for the long 12-mile hike into the bush was her six-week old pup.

"You'd be surprised how heavy a six weeks old pup can get."

Helen Leonard's job was clerk-dispatcher for the main ranger station there at Spirit Lake. Every two hours, she would contact the lookouts on Swift Creek, Coldwater and Strawberry peaks to the north of St. Helens. On the south side, her schedule included ringing Vanson and Mitchell peaks to see if the lookouts had fallen off a cliff.

Experienced with a compass and the fire finder, Helen practiced over the phone with her lookouts, trading map readings and "what if" scenarios. During Hazel's first few weeks at the remote lookout, Helen called her from the ranger station to practice sighting imaginary smoke on the horizon through the "gun" of her fire finder. "She kept me practicing maybe two or three times a day."

The phone was the vital link that civilized the woods for both men and women alike. Strung tree to tree, the phone wire crossed hills and creeks to lookout points near Mount Adams. The phones extended clear to Packwood and beyond to Mount Rainier. Along about six o'clock after the day's duties were done and the dishes had been cleared away, somebody on a peak up near Packwood would ring, requesting Helen to "Read us the funny paper. What is Betty Boop doing today?" Everybody on the line would answer and listen in.

"So I would read them the papers in the evening and all these people on these peaks around the mountains would listen. They weren't particularly interested in news but in the funny papers. They would exchange recipes too."

Days never dragged for Helen there at the ranger station. Nor did the nights. Bears filled the woods, especially towards dusk. One night, a yearling attacked the garbage can on her porch, spilling the soggy napkins and pork and bean cans all over the yard. Disgusted, she tore out snapping at the bear who hightailed it for the woods. After cleaning up the contents, she returned to her cabin. No more than a minute or two later, she heard rustling in the bushes and clang-clang there went the garbage can again.

Out she burst again to find the bear with his rear-end sticking out of the garbage can. With her broom still in hand, Helen lunged across the porch yelling at the creature twice her size. She took careful aim and swatted him once, twice, and again for good measure, whacking the bear over his back until he extricated himself. So astonished was he that this petite woman was viciously attacking him that the bear turned and ran down a little ravine beside the house, stopping only briefly to look around a stump to see if she was pursuing.

Helen thought a moment about what she was doing. A ranger in the cabin nearby opened his door to see what the racket was about. He shook his head. Helen reflected a moment about the danger she had exposed herself to and quickly retreated to her house.

Fires posed serious problems to the rangers there at Spirit Lake. Ranger Samuelson got the word quickly enough from the lookouts atop the various peaks throughout the district. Helen would give the precise locations to Samuelson. He had the equipment—shovels, water tanks, pick-axes and so on. But firefighters were few and inexperienced.

The solution during the war was to "make do." There was more than one weekend when campers staying at Spirit Lake were volunteered by Ranger Samuelson to pack in a few miles to fight a fire on some distant mountain ridge.

Jack Nelson, proprietor of Harmony Falls Lodge, came over with his boat and got firefighting equipment for his guests whenever a fire threatened his woods.

Fortunately, there were some conscientious objectors stationed at Wind River. They too were drafted for trail fire duty. They were exhausted from the long hike by the time they arrived at the fire, but they fought it anyway. Cloudy weather and the mountain dampness bailed out the Forest Service more than a few times, too.

The women on the lookouts did not get as lonely as the men. Boredom was the lookout's enemy. Hazel contracted the malady early but warded it off with long conversations with her puppy. And there was the lookout housework.

"When I got bored on cloudy days, when you couldn't do any looking, why, I painted the inside of that old lookout. I had 180 panes of glass, 360 if you count both sides. They all had to be washed every week. If you had a dust storm or a rainstorm, you had to do it oftener."

Hazel's particular lookout was a weather station. She checked and logged the temperature, humidity and the wind direction and velocity, twice a day.

Daily tasks included chopping wood into stove lengths for burning. An ancient tin stove with holes burned in the side served as the oven. Hazel made her own yeast bread and managed to whip together some pretty acceptable gingerbread too. Lack of refrigeration meant canned or packaged cuisine, but the chilly mountain air kept a chunk of bacon from going bad as long as Hazel stored it in the cooler on the lookout tower catwalk.

Water was another chore for Hazel. Men usually carried five gallons at a time from a spring a quarter of a mile down below the lookout. Hazel could manage three gallons up the hill and the 12 steps of her lookout ladder. Three gallons lasted her a day.

"Of course, I had that pup. It was no easy job to housebreak a pup when you are 15 feet off the ground. She kept me pretty busy."

Evenings, Hazel was so tired she ignored the gasoline lantern and the candles in favor of sack time. Sleep came easily. One night, however, she tightened up at the sound of sniffing outside the lookout tower door. Hazel pulled herself together and thought momentarily of checking out her visitor.

"I thought maybe it was a bear after the bacon I had in that box. I didn't look out because I thought maybe I'd be happier if I didn't know what it was."

Suddenly, that little pup zipped across the floor, nearly colliding with the door. She barked loudly. Then the lookout tower swayed as whatever it was sprang off the catwalk.

The next morning, Hazel climbed down to inspect her premises. Sunlight bathed the clearing in its usual nippy glow at this altitude. To Hazel's great horror, she found several round cougar tracks the size of her hand in the pumiceous soil around the tower.

The trail workers came by often that summer with loads of pre-cut firewood for Hazel. She enjoyed her woods but she always welcomed company too.

To be alive in these woods was for Hazel Marcellus an opportunity that she would take advantage of again the next summer and the summer after that. Everybody should have such an opportunity. She was surrounded by views of Mount Hood to the far southeast, Adams to the east and Rainier to the northeast. And there was Mount St. Helens, the "Lady" itself, always there, right there, present and not to be ignored.

"I could practically reach out and touch Mount St. Helens, it was so close. I was just kind of in this cup with all these beautiful mountains around. I'm glad I had the experience."

World War II created the opportunity Hazel enjoyed. After the war, life returned to normal for her and the millions of other Americans who had "made do" for the war effort. Schoolteaching would never quite be the same though.

For Helen, the end of World War II was especially memorable. Her supervisor was up from Vancouver, Washington. Everybody had to bustle around, picking up trash, raking the beds, straightening parking barriers and bracing for inspection. A thunderstorm came in the midst of the visit by the supervisor. And then word reached Spirit Lake that the war was ended. All personnel could have two days off!

Well, the supervisor decided he would spend his two days vacation at Spirit Lake. Helen and the troops were feeling slightly put-upon, when suddenly she spotted a ribbon of smoke on Bear Pass. She quickly rousted all available personnel and under the watchful eye of the supervisor they headed for the lightning fire, shovels and picks in hand. Hooray! The war was over.

Chapter IX

Ole's Secret

Forty years ago, before bulldozers cleared the land and the electric company dammed up the Lewis River, a hermit named Ole Peterson accepted the logic of frugality. How he lived impressed campers and hikers who stopped for a dipper full of water. Why Ole chose his remote existence remains a mystery.

Ole's choice to live alone in the woods was odd, even by turn-of-the-century standards. He shared his cabin with his chickens. His bulls roamed the woods in pursuit of their pleasure. He had tobacco and onions hanging from the ceiling of his one-room shack. He cut the beams himself and then cured them a honey brown with the accumulation of 50 years of pipe smoke and bacon grease.

In the front window was a little bench with his washbowl. In every nook and cranny of the room, dust covered the cobwebs abandoned by many generations of spiders. A perpetually hot potbellied stove that eventually led to Ole's downfall maintained a steady vigil in the middle of the room.

Ole saved every newspaper he had ever brought in from Woodland, some 40 miles west by trail. The newspapers were stacked from floor to ceiling all the way around the room, two and three rows deep towards the center. They attested in their crumbling yellow way to the folly of mankind that Ole sought to avoid way out there in the woods.

The walls of Ole's shack were wallpapered with campaign posters of William McKinley, 25th president of the United States from 1897 until he was assassinated in 1901. Ole agreed with the politics of McKinley — a Republican! There is no telling how much deeper into the wilderness Ole would have retreated if Democrat William Jennings Bryan or, God-forbid, Prohibitionist John C. Woolley had won.

Outside his cabin, Ole's garden thrived while Republicans occupied the White House and suffered during reigns of the dreaded Democrats. He hated Democrats. His political opinions became widely known during the 1930s when Skamania County decided there were enough voters in the upper Lewis area to create a precinct. Ole's house was selected as the polling station. When the women from the county clerk's office arrived, Ole welcomed them with fanfare befitting the occasion and granted them the run of his estate.

Typewriters, old phonographs, newspapers, half-buried furniture, and an amazing amount of junk everywhere prompted the ladies to shake their heads in disbelief more than disapproval. They immediately set to work, carving out polling booths amidst a sea of newsprint.

Meanwhile, two of the women took the hot coffeepot off the stove and tiptoed out of the door. They chortled at the sign Ole had posted over the door: "No damned Democrats allowed." Then they dumped the coffeepot. It was filled to within two inches of the top with ancient coffee grounds and the remains of dozens of eggshells, which prevented murkiness in the coffee. Years of brewing had cured the insides black. No amount of scouring could make it shine, but at least the pot was clean.

The ladies were all set to handle the trickle of voters expected that day and they were feeling pretty warm inside for the service they had rendered Ole when the hermit glided through the front door. Face aglow, he headed for his old coffeepot. Suddenly, his usually sunny temperament turned cold. A sheet of ice formed on his face. He asked what in blazes had the women done.

"You've ruined my coffeepot. You've ruined it. Get out of my house!" Then he kicked the whole election committee out the front door.

Ironically, Ole may have had pretty good reason for his opinion of Democrats, especially of President Franklin D. Roosevelt and his New Deal. During the 1930s, the U.S. Forest Service literally took a patch of Ole's land and built a Civilian Conservation Corps camp. The confiscation was unintended. The CCC thought it was on Forest Service land. Ole was angry, but did nothing. The CCC and its parent, the U.S. Forest Service, felt uncomfortable, though. In 1942, the Forest Service's K.P. Cecil charged Ranger Jim

Langdon with the task of approaching Ole and talking him into signing a lease of his land to the government.

Ole was already mad about the encroachment. Besides, he had unsuccessfully argued that some of the CCCs should re-roof his shack since they were working for taxpayers anyway. The CCC boss had not felt the request exactly fitting and refused.

By the time Langdon was assigned to the job, there reportedly had been several incidents in which Ole had run off government people with his gun. He mellowed though after a few negotiating sessions with Langdon, especially after the ranger agreed to partake of Ole's home-brewed beer. Langdon shut his eyes, strained the brew through his teeth as best he could and gulped. It was only because of Langdon's high sense of duty that the Forest Service finally got its lease from Ole Peterson.

Big old maples dotted Ole's acreage. Moss clung to the hardwoods for dear life. Ole prized the beauty of his shack on the river and refused to sell off the timber in hopes that his property might be turned into a youth camp some day.

North of Ole's spot in the woods was a vast system of 37 lava caves created by Mount St. Helens during a particularly fluid pique 1,900 years ago. The names intrigued many a hiker who asked directions from Ole: Bat, Spider, Utterstrom's, Dollar, Dime, Beaver, Flow and, of course, Ole's Cave.

Ole's Cave was special. The big-eared Townsend's bat and other bat species congregated inside the vast lava tube by day. Salamanders crept about in the coolness of night. Ole discovered his cave in 1895. For a small fee, and sometimes for free, he conducted tours. Visitors often stayed overnight in a small log house adjacent to the the cave's lower entrance.

Brothers Don and Allen Cripe climbed and hiked around Mount St. Helens half a century and were friends of Ole Peterson.

"Thirty to 35 years ago, I was in the caves. We stayed at Ole Peterson's place. He fed us that night. We went through the caves. We had cameras with us and got flash pictures right inside the caves," said Allen. He recalled too his impression of Ole.

"I would say that he was more or less a person who liked to be by himself. He didn't like to be around people and you could call him a hermit. He was a person who liked to be around the animals, around nature. He reminded me something of this fellow you see on television, Grizzly Adams. Animals lived around his place. They weren't scared of him. They all knew him. That was the type of person he was."

Photographer and amateur botanist Franz Gunnar Nilsson often visited Ole during the 1930s and 1940s. He borrowed a kerosene lantern from the old hermit to light his way in Ole's Cave. His memory of Ole is crystalline.

"I first saw him in the late 1930s. From then on I kept visiting off and on.

"Ole liked to buy cars but never drove them. I don't know if he went to town to buy them. He had a shed with half a dozen or more new cars. He would just bring them up and let them sit in the shed. That was as far as they would go.

"I guess everybody was interested in his cars. He liked to show them and he liked to talk politics. He was a sharp old cookie. Even though he was a hermit, he liked to see people come around.

"If you went into his place in the wintertime, the chickens lived in his kitchen with him. I remember one time I went up there with a watermelon. We ate half of it. The other half I gave to Ole. In return, he wanted to give me a loaf of his bread. I took the bread, but I didn't eat it because all those chickens and one thing and another was hanging around his kitchen.

"I don't think he ever took his clothes off because his rubber boots were taped to his pants. He had a cot and laid down when he got tired. I think he must have been in his eighties towards the end. He was always cheerful and always smiling."

There was a basket ferry across the Lewis River right above Ole's cabin. Hikers into the area parked their vehicles on the road nearby. They shuttled across the Lewis in the basket to a riverbank trailhead on the other side en route to Mitchell Peak. The area was wild. Bear pawed about menacingly. Cougar eyed hare from dense thickets. Deer and elk wintered in the area. Ole prowled the region the way an animal did, sometimes in search of food, sometimes just curious. He knew the Forest Service and was allowed to gossip over their primitive phone system strung from tree to tree between fire lookout stations. Hazel Marcellus was high atop Mitchel Peak when her phone set would ring. Sometimes, it was Ole.

"He used to call me up when I was up there on Mitchell. He talked to me and asked me about how I was and what I was doing, that sort of thing.

"I said it was all fine except for the thunderstorms."

Ole said, "Oh, that's where thunder is born."

Ole made no secret that he liked all animals, but his chickens were his best friends. Every night, he would get up on a stump and circle around and around, leading the chickens with a steady dribble of feed. They scratched and pecked, scratched and pecked, until they were galloping around the stump like a carousel in miniature with Ole as its centerpiece.

Ole's love and respect for animals, wild and domesticated, was not always in line with generally accepted principles of husbandry. Area residents thought he was nuts. Again, Forest Service Ranger Jim Langdon had to tangle with Ole. The imbroglio was not without its humorous aspects.

"He had a bunch of cattle. He didn't believe a bull should ever be deprived of his pleasures of life. So he would never neuter them. They always were running around there—full bull. During the war, people started moving up the valley and logging started to move in there. Some of these old bulls were getting a bit mean. The ladies were pretty much housebound because the bulls wouldn't let them out of the house. They were scared of them. So there was a bit of agitation.

"Ole says, 'I'm not going to do nothing to the bulls.' Rupe Ward and I finally convinced Ole that maybe he should do something about them. We bought them (and) butchered a couple of them for Ole. We got some of the meat and he took some.

"He put this meat away for himself. How the old boy ever lived, I don't know. He ground it up and put it in a 10-gallon crock. He put a layer of ground meat in there, a layer of salt, a layer of ground meat, a layer of salt. And good Lord, when I saw the keg in the spring after it had set all winter, it stunk to the heaven. It was green. And he was still eating the stuff. I couldn't believe it."

Ole's reputation preceded him. Many people were afraid of the old hermit. The fear was unwarranted. Helen M. Leonard, clerk-dispatcher for the Spirit Lake Ranger Station, recalls her first impression of Ole as a bit hair-raising.

"Our bosses kind of dared us girls to go over there. So we went over and Ole invited us into his house, for which I've always been thankful. It was really something you would never see ever again."

Ole's world started coming down around him after World War II with the influx of hikers and campers using the newly constructed roads into the once-pristine wilderness area. No longer was he isolated. Developers sought his land, too, as the site for the new dam that would form Swift Creek Reservoir. His little ramshackled cabin stood back then where today the road crosses the Swift Creek Reservoir diversion channel.

Whether Ole would have given up his home in the woods, no one will ever know. Fire erupted inside his small shack, loaded with flammable bric-a-brac from the past 75 years. Ole was out of the building but decided to rush back in and rescue something precious in his life. The roof fell in on him. He was severely burned. Friends rushed him to the hospital for treatment. Time ran out on Ole Peterson, though. He died in a hospital bed.

Why Ole abandoned our rich culture with its vast storehouse of knowledge and tools, cars and consumer goods, we can only guess. He understood technology, that is certain. He was a good Republican, deeply affected by McKinley's assassination in 1901. He cared for the tall timber, for his chickens and his bulls. He marvelled at the lava tubes and his ability to get two bits for a tour through them. He set himself apart from his fellow man because he no longer cared to set himself apart from nature. He left Woodland seeking his place within the natural order. And somehow, he sustained himself. Perhaps, therein lies Ole's secret.

Chapter X

Coming of Age at Spirit Lake

For years, girls attended the Portland YWCA's Camp Westwind down on the Salmon River in Oregon. Then came Pearl Harbor and the blackout years of World War II forcing the "Y" to move its summer sessions to Spirit Lake.

Beatrice Heskett with crisply marcelled gray hair headed up the kitchen for the "Y" at Camp Westwind. She realized the move to Spirit Lake would be difficult but the reward of waking up to the reflection of Mount St. Helens in Spirit Lake would make the trip worth it. Beatrice asked a 15-year-old girl named Patty Otis if she might like to go too as her kitchen helper.

The job both frightened and tempted Patty. Mrs. Heskett was an old family friend. But it would be Patty's first extended trip out of the fruit and nut farm area of the Willamette Valley in western Oregon. She was so shy.

"I remember how lonely I felt, boarding the big Greyhound bus at the "Y" where everyone seemed to know each other and all the camp songs and games."

Patty bounced along in the bus pondering her dilemma. Why had she allowed herself to be persuaded to spend the summer away from that solid, secure home in which she grew up? Little did she know that "kitchen helper" was a position reserved by the YWCA for needy kids out of Depression homes that lacked money for camp tuition. Soon Patty spied Mount St. Helens, the snowcapped peak under which she would be spending the summer. Larger and larger on the horizon it grew, a delectable scoop of ice cream on a volcanic cone, melting under the already hot summer skies of 1942.

The open road gave Patty a perfect view of the countryside. Then, quite suddenly, the bus lurched through an opening in a dense wall of great Douglas firs and ancient cedars. The mountain disappeared. The sun disappeared. The road went crooked. Patty peered out the window, subdued, while the rest of the girls yakked and sang strange camp songs with which she was unfamiliar. The hours slipped by before a din of recognition welled up in the front of the bus and rippled down the aisle seats: "There it is!"

Spirit Lake popped out of the woods. It was just there, calm except for some cat's paw wavelets kicked up by the warm gusts of wind. Patty looked for Mount St. Helens. It was gone, absolutely gone, from sight. Being on the south side of the lake with the tall timber to their backs, Patty and the rest of the YWCA campers would have to wait until they were a quarter mile across the lake before they would be able to see St. Helens once again.

The adults barked orders to the girls to load this, sit there, move that, get going, until all their gear was packed onto a huge open barge, ready for towing across the lake. The girls harmonized in "Tell Me Why." Then it happened:

"I watched the sight I shall never forget. Mount St. Helens began to rise above the ridge of blue-black trees. I watched her emerge. In awe and surprise, I wept."

Her crying continued for three days, though not for the same reason. Patty grew homesick, violently yearning for the security of her valley home. She was late for meals or tried to skip them altogether. One blonde-haired counselor, Bernie Askey, a perceptive girl from Omaha, found her out.

"You see, for the first three days I was either crying, throwing up or having violent diarrhea, and became well acquainted with the three outhouses, Hewey, Louie and Dewey."

Bernie insisted Patty come to breakfast early enough to eat some of the hot cereal.

"That hot cereal settled my system. I became a real camper after that meal."

Patty's kitchen duties were pretty light. She set the tables, peeled carrots, cut fruit and directed the campers assigned KP that day. When Bliss Clark found out Patty could push a wheelbarrow without tipping it over, he had her hauling items for him. On most days, though, there was time for swimming practice so Patty could pass the rowboat test.

Passing her swim test opened up a new world to Patty. Once she earned the right to go boating, she started rowing alone from Camp Meehan on the northern bank of Spirit Lake over to Harmony Falls Lodge to pick up the mail. There she bumped into Jack Nelson, a huge man who seemed to swoop down from the sky when he turned his bemused gaze on her. Jack's sister Ruby and his wife Tressa yelled "Hallo!" and offered her cold drinks when Patty came for the day's mail. Camp was turning out not to be so bad after all.

Soon, Patty was wearing her red deer hunting hat, borrowed from her Dad. A jaunty coon tail dangled from the back of the hat, befitting her newfound high spirits.

The YWCA camp leaders pondered poor Patty's plight: Much of her first week had been a disaster. They decided to award her a scholarship for a week of freedom from kitchen duties. She could participate fully as a camper. Delighted at the propsects, Patty moved her belongings from the cook's cabin down to Goat Mountain cabin where she took top bunk. Her cabin mates were Muriel, Marilu and Barbara.

Day began at 7:30 a.m. with reveille. After a hot breakfast, there were work groups, then maybe a hike or waterfront activity. Cabins took turns at KP. There was supposed to be no drudgery at Camp Meehan. Those working on the most mundane, boring chores, were supposed to burst into cheerful song:

> Oh, sing along
> At work or while at play
> Though skies are gray
> And dull the day
> Just sing along the way

"Sing-A-Long" was to be repeated until the chore was done, which quite soon it was.

There were the mysterious mines in the region: Lange's Mine. Coe's Mine. How had mere mortals been able to transport the rusting donkey engine to the once-thriving mine site? And why? Gold fever? Copper?

The hike to Donnybrook Camp on the east bank of Spirit Lake, a quarter of a mile southwest of Cedar Creek Forest Camp, resolved the burning question raised by the girls the first day they barged across the lake: "Which camp appeared first?" The hike around the lake on the moccasin-soft pumaceous trail revealed which of the girls knew her shoreline best. Such knowledge of Spirit Lake marked a girl for life, or at least until the end of summer.

The hike up to Meta Lake produced the heartiest girls in the bunch.

"We were taught the hiking skill of turning to face downhill when standing to rest to allow leg muscles to relax."

Patty also learned the system of counting miles hiked by picking up pumiceous stones the size of her little finger every so often, then exchanging so many stones for a leaf. Ten leaves equalled a mile.

The hike most special in Patty's memory was led by camp director Gwenn Retherford, out for the summer from Ferndale, Michigan. She led the girls up to timberline shortly after sunrise and read them "The Creation." Again, Patty wept.

During each session, the counselors got a day off to visit the Nelsons at Harmony Falls. Patty was chosen to replace Gwenn as honorary acting camp director.

Gwenn took Patty's coon tail cap. Patty wore Gwenn's familiar jacket and whistle that hung from a braided lanyard. The day went smoothly and the campfire smoke that evening blew straight up to the sky. Gwenn usually closed the campfire each night. That night, Patty and the girls stood for the closing friendship circle, each holding the hand of her neighbor in the dark, singing:

> When the call of the fire comes to us through the shadows that
>   follow the close of the day
> It brings us a peace and a calmness of spirit that drives all our
>   troubles away
> We're thankful for days and the joys that they bring us
> For nights and the rest that they bring.
> May we go on believing in this love we're receiving
> Just now 'round the fire as we sing.

There was a moment of silence, followed by the closing portion of the song:

> Come all, say goodnight
> While the shadows fade into the evening light
> In each living blowing ember
> There are friendships to remember
> So we say one last goodnight.
> Good night . . . to you.

Then Patty said softly, "Good night campers." As she did, she firmly squeezed the hand of the camper next to her, starting an electric current of friendship that sped around the circle of clasped hands.

Absolute silence was expected as they filed back to their cabins through the darkening woods. Taps.

The counselors returned to camp from their day-long adventure at Harmony Falls with dozens of stories and anecdotes about Jack Nelson. His name was legendary around the camp, indeed all Spirit Lake, after the first few weeks of every summer session. The counselors talked about his fishing exploits, his encounters with bears, his grim warnings of monsters lurking in the deeps of Spirit Lake or high above in the snowy passes of Mount St. Helens. Nelson was the proprietor of the lodge, but he was something of an expert on tall tales, too.

Finally, one evening, it was arranged for Jack to come across the lake and tell around the campfire about the hairy apes of Mount St. Helens.

"They'll steal away all the red-headed campers," he said, scaring the wits out of the unlucky few with auburn red hair. Big Jack looked at Patty and her cabinmates and warned that they would know the apes were around if large rocks crashed on the roof of Goat Mountain cabin.

Sure enough, that evening rocks crashed on the cabin roof. Through the windows, Patty and the girls stared wide-eyed at hideous creatures with angry red cheeks, resembling the effect created by a flashlight stuck in a human's mouth. The creatures warned the girls not to go to Ape Canyon, which by coincidence was the hike destination scheduled for the next day.

Sundays were special. Manners were taught and enforced every day, but especially on Sunday. Chicken and potatoes were received in the right hand, transferred to the left, and passed on to your neighbor. Never, never did Patty or the girls touch a fork until the head of the table did.

On Sunday, each camper dressed in her whitest shirt and shorts with a sky-blue Girl Reserve neckerchief tied around her neck. They filed down to the lake shore for church services on driftwood logs, facing Mount St. Helens across the lake.

Patty, Marilu and Alice were assigned Sunday services in August that summer. Patty's duty was to present the sermon, an intellectual task as difficult as any she had ever had.

Pencil in hand, she thought about the chattering girls on the barge with her that first day she arrived at Spirit Lake. She mulled over those Harmony Falls rowboat trips for mail. The quiet. Campfires were raucous with laughter and singing and Jack Nelson's storytelling, but the peacefulness of the Mount Margaret backcountry made the place special. Patty focused on the wilderness around her. The people, all her new friends, were special. So were the stories and songs, games and group hikes. But it was this quiet wilderness that made the experience for Patty Otis, age 15, in the summer of '42.

The campers entered in silence and sat in their places. The choir struck up "The Lord is in His holy temple: let all the earth keep silence before Him."

Patty's roommate, Marilu, recited her poem, "Silence," followed by the hymn, "Peace, I Ask Of Thee, Oh River." Then it was Patty's turn:

"Why Silence?"

Silence — nothing tangible.
Nothing in material form,
Nothing you can reach out your hand towards and say:
"Here is a piece of silence I gathered while in the cool forest shade
 yesterday."
Then why, in this fast-moving world,
Where days are packed with activities,
Where realities make up a day,
Why do we remember and seek silence?
Why do we place value on something that isn't there?
Why do tall trees press forward into the sky and reach their green
 arms into the heavens?
Why do nighthawks soar up into the sunset?
Why do stalwart mountains stand strong against storms, year after
 year,
Piercing the blue with their snow-encrusted crowns?
Because God is there.
Because God speaks to us through silence.
For when we are in silence, we are in God's temple.
That is why we know and love ... silence.

Chapter XI

Snowcat Days and Ski Club Nights

There were no teetotalers and fewer cowards in the Longview Ski Club in 1953. Maybe that is why Harry Truman and his wife Eddie took such a liking to the members.

The club evolved from a six-mile hike Rex West and some friends made in 1936. From the road, West and his crew hiked through snowy brush and undergrowth until they reached the velvety white slopes of St. Helens. They hoped to find a ski area closer than Mount Hood in Oregon to the southeast and Mount Rainier far off to the northeast. On this day, they found dry snow and ideal ski conditions.

The only snag was the long hike. A year later, West skied in from the Dry Gulch area with a member of the U.S. Forest Service to locate a site for an official Longview Ski Club cabin. After resolving a mixup over the Northern Pacific's land boundary, West and Dan Phillips leased the land for the club from the government. Jay Miller, the carpenter in the group, designed the cabin to meet with the government's standards and strong enough to withstand 10 and 20 foot snowdrifts.

With the warmer weather in the summer of 1937, members of the newly formed club built the cabin, the first and only such dwelling to be located at timberline. The Forest Service loaned the club a team of mules to drag the cedar shake bolts they had split from the lake area to the cabin site three miles up the hill. West handled much of the carpentry. Brothers Don and Allen Cripe pitched in packing the lumber up the mountain and over the trail to the cabin site.

"I was in on hauling lumber up there. Harry (Truman) had the old place at the lake. We got to his lodge with our trailer of lumber and we went over to Harry's and sat on his back porch. I used to love to sit there and drink beer. And we got loaded with beer. We didn't make it to the cabin that night," said Don Cripe.

"We got about two-thirds of the way and decided to stop the car and sleep right there," said his brother Allen. The next morning, the haul was no easier. Indeed, the road got rougher until eventually there was no road at all.

"In fact, I ruined a Ford car hauling (that) trailer of lumber," Don recalled.

The cabin proved a godsend on cold days and colder nights. Cost of materials, mainly lumber, was $75. Their labor was free.

"It had an upstairs, kind of an attic with a ladder. It held about six bunks below and there was a kitchen. We had a stove in there. Above, we had army cots. I think you could get about six people upstairs, no more than 12 at the most. It was a simple cabin, rough sawn lumber," recalled Gunnar Nilsson, a cross-country skier and the unofficial club photographer.

"It was a rustic place, I'll tell you. You had to melt your snow to get your water. We burned Presto logs. In the fall of the year when we had work parties, they always brought Presto logs in," said Don Cripe. Despite the stove and the Presto logs, temperatures in the uninsulated cabin hovered at freezing on many a cold winter evening.

The ski clubbers christened the lodge on New Year's Day, 1938. They packed in a roast turkey and appropriate libations for the occasion. The New Year's parties became a tradition that Harry Truman and his wife Eddie joined in. Rob Quoidbach, an early ski club member recalled the lessons taught by his friend, the pedantic Truman.

"He and Eddie would come up and visit us on the New Year's Eve parties. We had a ball listening to Harry talk. Once he gets loaded, he was quite a talker. He had quite a few tales to tell, but the problem was that he kept telling them over and over."

With a cabin, the club attracted new members but never developed much beyond a looseknit organization of men and women who climbed Mount St. Helens and skied its slopes. They celebrated their achievements with loud parties in the club lodge. Rarely did their ranks number more than three dozen, though outsiders were always welcome.

In addition to the Wests, Nilssons and Cripes, there were Rob and Val Quoidbach, brothers known for their mountain climbing abilities; Don Bascom, the metal fabricator and entrepreneur of the group; and used car salesman George Bowers whose tongue rivaled that of Truman's.

Bascom made a welded steel sign for the club lodge door that said, "Don't break in. Join the ski club." The sign held the door together and helped cut down on vandalism in later years. Bascom also befriended Mount St. Helens Lodge owner Harry Truman by making him a fireplace andiron in the form of a tree with limbs.

Bascom's greatest contribution to the ski club community was his vision and the size of his wallet. Bascom, and to a lesser extent Val Quoidbach, bought a Tucker snowmobile in 1947. Equipped with skis in front and some rotating pontoons on the rear, the snowcat hauled members up the old timberline road to the ski club cabin and then towed people up the slopes. Four skiers fit in the cab with another 10 hanging on to ropes behind.

Previously, Bascom and some others had operated a rope tow at the 3,000 foot level near Spirit Lake Lodge. Called Woodpecker's Paradise because of the plethora of stumps, the towing operation was a commercial failure. The snow was too wet and sticky. With the snowcat, Bascom and Quoidbach generated interest in skiing at the higher 4,000 to 6,000 foot elevations.

Interest in skiing snowballed. The ski club even bought a little portable gasoline engine, head and tail pulleys and a sheave. Rex West scrounged tow rope from Longview Fibre where he was a mill foreman. They dubbed the contraption erected on a hillside the Sweden Rope Tow. An addition to the cabin became necessary, too.

"I helped build the addition. We made our own shakes. Underneath were cedar logs. We didn't have any cement. Their weather up there is such that things dry out pretty good. It was windy. There was no problem of rotting," said Nilsson. If things got too frigid, the club repaired to Harry Truman's lodge down below.

Truman and his wife Eddie hosted parties at their Mount St. Helens Lodge for the club members on weekends. The wily Truman's growing interest in the snowcat paralleled Bascom's soaring popularity among the skiers. Occasionally, Bascom would comment about the trouble the engine might be giving him or the harrowing experience he had climbing a steep grade. Bascom enjoyed the snow, too, so driving the cat prevented him from charging down the hills on skis. Truman led into Bascom's comments with his own thoughts about taking the cat off his hands. Soon Truman had sold himself on the cat as a money-maker rivaling his rowboats in the summer. Before the

101

negotiating was settled, Truman popped for $4,000 in 1952 to buy the cat from Bascom and Quoidbach.

The next year promised to be fantastic. Truman allowed the skiers to install a phone from timberline to his lodge with a large sign that read, "Phone for Sno-Cat." He charged $2 for the one-way trip. Truman gradually realized that the three-mile trip from his lodge to the timberline cabin was repetitious and not very profitable unless he had a full cab and five or six on the ropes behind the cat. His temper occasionally boiled over. Sometimes he would shrug his shoulders if a group wanted to go up the hill or pretend he did not hear the phone if club members called to come down. Gunnar Nilsson recalled the dilemma:

"I know Truman was a hard cookie to get along with. You had to watch Truman because you could say the wrong thing and he would fly off the handle.

"If Truman wanted to haul you up, okay. But if he didn't, then to hell with you. You were never sure whether you were going to get a ride up there. So, I thought, there's a way to cure this.

"I suggested we make Harry Truman an honorary member of the ski club, for life. We made a big certificate, gold seal on it, and all that English style of writing. We all threw a party up at Truman's—must have been about 15 or 20 of the ski club members. When Truman saw it, he cried. Harry never refused us a ride after that. Of course, we had to pay for it still."

Skiing dominated wintertime activities of the club, though the members were natural athletes who climbed the mountain year-round. Cross-country skiing opportunities were abundant but few clubbers were interested in the scenery.

"We weren't interested in distance. We were interested in speed. We would hike up the hill and ski down and pant all the way back up again. The fun was going up on the back of the Dogs Head. It took about an hour to hike up there and you could ski down in 10 minutes, or so," said Rob Quoidbach.

Skiing ungroomed slopes on an unpredictable mountain like St. Helens had its drawbacks, too. In the wintertime, a soft, light snow would blow off the ridges, leaving them bare and icy. The ravines would fill with soft snow. Skiers deceived by the powder would hit those ridges and wipe out like a rock skipping over the water.

Spring skiing at the higher elevations a couple thousand feet from the summit proved exceptional when the ridges were coated with corn snow.

By far, the most dangerous skiing—and most exhilarating—was from the 9,677-foot summit of Mount St. Helens. There were no chairlifts to the top. The descent began only after several hours of mountainclimbing. Club members would lay their skis flat on the snow, cross one tip over the other and tie them together with a sash cord, which was looped to the climber's belt. The skis were dragged up the mountain. Carrying them would have been foolish.

Skiers carried their regular ski boots in their packs and wore their climbing boots. If there was fresh snow, the climb proceeded smoothly. If the way became icy, climbers had to stop and pull on their crampons. The act of putting on crampons was discouraging to the would-be skiers because it signaled the end of the ski expedition. Crampons meant that conditions were too unsafe for skiing. If a person attempted to ski down St. Helens on ice, and fell, the rest of the climbing party might as well form a search party to pick up the pieces. Allen Cripe recalled the many, many times he was halted by ice close to the summit. "I haven't gotten them to the top more than four or five times," he said.

Skiing down a 9,677-foot mountain does have its rewards though. Cripe remembered one of his descents this way:

"The experience is quite something because you only live it just once — the first sensation. The first hundred yards off the mountain is a fairly gradual slope. When you reach the point where it breaks over between the Arrowhead and the Boot up there, you can't see.

"It breaks over so steep that you can't see actually where you are going. When you do get right on the edge, you stand there and say about four or five Hail Mary's.

"It takes a lot of nerve to make the first turn. You are looking straight down on the outside of the turn. When you make a turn and the object is not to fall, you have to make parallel turns. It is too steep to make any other type of turns, stem turns or anything."

The ultimate ski challenge was met by Rob Quoidbach and Allen Cripe. The two hearty mountaineers skied down 5,000 feet of elevation from the summit to the club cabin at timberline. Normal ski time was an hour and a half. They have made the plunge in 20 minutes.

Many have fallen and a few have died on Mount St. Helens. The arctic conditions alone can kill a man. Even the best, and that includes Rob Quoidbach and the legendary Jake Jones, have taken their falls. Quoidbach fell 1,500 feet while skiing down St. Helens. Jones lost his ice axe, broke his tailbone and has an ugly scar on his elbow even today to attest to the braking effects he had to exert when he fell a couple thousand feet.

Add to the danger the churlish behavior of a brooding volcano. Don Cripe nearly lost his life merely traversing the summit of St. Helens one day. The Longview club members knew better than to walk from the north rim of the volcanic cone to the south. They always went around to the west to avoid the crevasses and fissures in the depression of the cone. On this particularly day, though, Cripe and his brother and some other climbers were a little too complacent:

"We signed the register. Everybody was pretty happy about making the climb. It had been nice and all of a sudden, boom! I just fell. It just let loose under my feet and I just fell. Thank God my crampons caught on the side. I was down almost to my shoulder and my neck. Howard McCorkle was a good mountaineer. He hollered right away for me not to move. They got a rope and pulled me out.

"I could look down and see blue ice down there. I don't think I would have cared to go down there at all. I often wondered how far it could have been down to the rocks and ice on the top of Mount St. Helens, through the snow and the glacier and ice and everything. It was mighty deep, right on the very top."

Nilsson remembered his own near-death experience too. Jake Jones was leading the climb when Nilsson suddenly slipped through a snow bridge and was suspended in mid-air over a crevasse too deep to throw back an echo.

"They pulled me out. I said, 'Now do you think we should rope up?' And of course we did."

Jones was less a skier, more an outdoorsman and mountain climber. He drew contour lines for Weyerhaeuser five days a week, then spent his weekends getting some exercise climbing Mount St. Helens, sometimes twice in one day. He carried on the mountaineer traditions established by Lige Coalman, John C. Meehan and Grandpa Robert C. Lange before him. Don Cripe recalled the example Jones set for him personally:

"I gained a lot of courage on Mount St. Helens. One of the first trips I climbed with Jake Jones was horrendous. I was scared. I froze. Jake would get me going again and I would freeze again. Later on, not that I'm trying to brag or anything, but you gain confidence. I don't know what it is, but I got so I could run around the mountain quite free of fear."

The bonds among the ski club members and others who camped, hiked, fished and climbed around Mount St. Helens were casual and informal. The lodge cabin was open to the public. Use was not restricted and membership in the club was, while encouraged, not mandatory.

"The ski cabin in later years had been used probably more by outsiders than ski club members. We have made it available, and were supposed to make it available, to other groups. The Boy Scouts and the Penguin Hiking Club from Vancouver have used it," said West.

The ski club and its associates influenced the lodges and the youth camps in the area. Members felt a kinship, especially with the youth camps.

"I used to take the Longview YMCA boys up the mountain. Val and Rob Quoidbach, both of them, we would change off. I'd take them one year and then Rob might take them the next year, and then maybe Val would take them," recalled Jones.

When U.S. Supreme Court Justice William O. Douglas attempted to climb the mountain in 1953, he was accompanied by Rob and Val Quoidbach of the ski club and Bob McCall of the Mount St. Helens Ski Patrol and Search and Rescue Unit, which Val had helped establish five years earlier. Val remembered his instructions to the letter: "No matter what happens," read a telegram received from Washington, D.C., before starting the ascent, "Justice Douglas is to be taken care of first. Douglas must come off the mountain alive and well."

The ski club members knew well Jack Nelson, proprietor of Harmony Falls, his wife Tressa and sister Ruby. Recalled Jones:

"I called over there one day and by golly, I didn't any more than hang up and I looked way over there and he had his launch coming right at me. That was Jack Nelson. That's how I met him. I fell in love with him. He was sort of a Gary Cooper type, tall and had a bronze complexion."

U.S. Forest Ranger Harold "Sam" Samuelson and his staff represented the best sort of governmental regulation. Sam kept everything in line. A gentle spirit himself, he got along well with everybody.

The assorted miners and trappers in the area, especially George Brunk and Curly Hill, befriended the ski club crew. Brunk was Jake Jones' favorite climbing companion, after his own brothers, Alden and Clark.

"Gus" Gustafson, proprietor of Spirit Lake Lodge and son-in-law to Spirit Lake pioneer prospector Robert C. Lange, was a friend to the ski club as well. Recalled West:

"His family, the Lange family, had the restaurant there on the old highway. We always stopped by for huckleberry pie and coffee. The restaurant was still operated in 1938 when we built the cabin. That kept our body and soul together."

They laughed, they feuded, they watched over each other's places when need be. Harry Truman resolved one of his famous feuds with the Cripe brothers in order to protect his fishing boat rental business. Truman and the Cripes had had words. The reason for the argument has been forgotten. Nevertheless, to show his renewed friendship, Truman offered the boys free use of a boat and motor to show he wanted to be friends again. His motives were more complex, though. Recalled Don Cripe:

"Harry always kept track when we were up at the lake because he thought we always caught the big fish. This particular time—Harry always had his eye open for business—he said, 'Catch any fish, kids?' We said, 'Oh, yes, we've got a couple in our trunk.' We were getting ready to go and he said, 'No, you don't leave the lake now. People have been saying there are no fish in this lake. I lent you my poles and let you take the boat and the motor for free. I want some people to come down and see these fish.' He wanted to rent a few of his boats and get some fishermen out there."

The Longview Ski Club, like so many other organizations of people at Spirit Lake, was more a state of mind than an actual institution. The preoccupation of the people was with Mount St. Helens. The people associated with the ski club sold cars, worked in the woods or sawed lumber in nearby mills. Ordinary people. But their experiences, their vision, was extraordinary. Jake Jones could have been speaking for all ski club members, indeed, all Spirit Lake people:

"I thought Mount St. Helens was one of the most beautiful mountains in the world. I haven't been all over the world but I can't imagine seeing a prettier mountain.

"To see the sunrise from the top of Mount St. Helens was absolutely out of this world. It's just like dying and going to heaven, climbing at night and just sitting there, waiting and watching that sun come around the corner of Mount Adams. What a thrill! Mount St. Helens, I don't know, I fell in love with it. I don't think anybody loved it any more than I did."

Chapter XII

The Ghosts of Spirit Lake Lodge

Spirit Lake Lodge lay buried in the snowy forest of towering Douglas firs, shaggy pine and ancient cedar. Ice crusted up along the banks of the frozen Toutle River three feet from the lodge patio. A stillness clung to the air. Nothing breathed. A heavy darkness blanketed the snowy round shoulders of Mount St. Helens.

A warm yellow beam of life poured out from a single kerosene lantern perched on the window sill inside one of the second floor lodger's rooms above the main entrance. Inside that room two men talked.

"I'd say we chopped a good pile of wood today," said Harry Gustafson.

"Yeah, and now I guess we'll have to clean out that chimney before long," his companion replied.

Gustafson leaned back in his big leather rocking chair, gently massaging his arthritic elbow. Sitting across from the older Gustafson was Silas Scoggins, the lodge caretaker. Silas took care of the place through the long and lonesome winter months. Gustafson had ventured up the mountain to the lodge that afternoon to help Silas during the upcoming weekend when a few tourists might trek through the elements for some winter adventure.

Silas leaned back in his cane-bottomed chair and nodded, a little sleepy but deeply content from the chicken and gravy he had fried up earlier that evening. Harry's company was sure nice in the big, old lodge. Except for his shaggy black Labrador retriever — Bugsy — Silas had nobody to talk to other than himself during the weekdays. This was nice.

Bugsy curled up at Silas' feet, stood and walked in a tight circle, then lay down again and curled up. The big, long haired Lab must have weighed 150 pounds.

Gustafson smiled at the way the dog groaned and fell into a deep, restful sleep. He peered at Silas and asked about their neighbor, a fellow lodge owner up the road named Harry Truman.

"I seen how you and old Truman laid in a pretty big pile of wood. How'd you wangle that?" he asked Silas.

"Oh, me and Harry are buddies these days. He stopped in and asked me to help buck some logs down the road. He bribed some loggers to leave him a few in a ditch, but you know that old coot can sure make his case, especially when he's got a cooler full of six-packs," Silas laughed.

"Old Truman even made arrangements with the cutters there to cut him two-foot logs rather than chip 'em. We just drove down and hauled half back to his place and half to here," said Silas.

"How much did you get us?" Gustafson asked.

"Twenty cord," said Silas.

Gustafson whistled.

Suddenly, Bugsy's head popped up. His floppy ears stood straight up. Silas cocked his head sideways. Voices!

A woman said something about something somewhere.

A man's voice responded, "Yes."

Her voice went on, just barely out of earshot.

"What in the heck?" Silas could not quite make out what she was saying. Gustafson sat up, turned his head towards the bedroom door almost expecting somebody to walk in any moment.

"You hear that?" Silas asked.

"I think so," said Gustafson. "Maybe it's somebody got into the lodge?"

"No, no, couldn't be. I'm pretty sure I barred the front door and the back's snowed in clear to the eaves," Silas said. "I'm sure it's locked."

"You sure?" Gustafson asked once again. He could hear the woman clearly now. She was pointing out objects in the lodge to the man who would occasionally mutter, "Mmm, yes, yes. Mmm, yes."

Silas slid forward to the edge of his chair. "Yeah, I'm positive I wedged the shovel through the door handles. And I latched the top and the bottom of the door too. I'm sure I did."

Bugsy leaped to his feet and walked to the door. His nose reached up into the air, trying to catch a whiff of whoever, or whatever, was coming this way.

"You better go and take a look around," said Gustafson. Silas stood up and reached for his 410 shotgun leaning against the wall and a big, eight-battery flashlight on the top of a dresser drawer.

Gustafson's arthritis prevented him from jumping out of the big leather rocking chair. Silas pondered giving him a hand up, then decided to take a look-see by himself. "I'll be right back," he said.

Bugsy sprang to his feet as Silas reached for the doorknob. It turned ever so slightly. Silas recoiled. He pulled his hand back to the stock of the gun, gave it a pat, then reached out again to turn the knob.

"Here, take the lamp," said Gustafson, pointing to the kerosene lantern by the bed.

"Good idea," said Silas. It would be kind of hard juggling the flashlight, lantern and his shotgun, but pitch black and horrific without them.

"I'm coming now," Silas said to the intruders outside their bedroom door. He twisted the heavy, cast-iron knob, pushed open the solid wood door and blasted the full length of the hallway with the big flashlight. An eerie reflection off the picture frame at the far end of the hall blinded Silas for a second. He quickly scanned the hall with his lights. Shadows fled into the doorways to the seven other second-floor lodge rooms. He inched down the hallway, flashing inside each lodge room. In each was a handmade bed, its mattress carefully bunked over for the winter. Each room had a bone china kerosene lamp on the nightstand. The handpainted lampshades leered back at Silas, prompting him to hurry on to the next room.

"Come on, boy," said Silas to his dog. "Let's get this over with."

They paced down the long hallway the length of the lodge. Nothing here. Nothing there. The voices seemed more remote. The mysterious man and woman must have disappeared downstairs to the main lodge area, somewhere near the stairwell, or maybe they were lurking in the basement.

"Hello! down there?" Silas called out.

Silas edged closer to the stairs, threw the beam of light from his powerful flashlight down below and brought into full view two red, white and blue wooden Indian heads.

Creeeeak! Creeeeak! Creeeeak! went the steps as he descended, Bugsy by his side, strangely unwilling to bolt downstairs.

At the landing, Silas checked the dark edges of the room and placed the kerosene lantern on the end of the bannister. He levelled the flashlight and probed the shadowy forms frozen around the lobby. Salt shakers cowered behind napkin holders on each of five dining tables. Ghastly images smiled out of burled myrtlewood picture frames that lined the walls above the antique end tables. There was no phone.

Stale candy and spools of fishing line gleamed behind the cut glass showcases. Silas angled to the left and passed the horseshoe bar and grill area in the middle of the lodge. No voices now, but a heavy sigh of air exhaled from the flue of the woodstove at the top of the stairs. Bugsy paid it no mind, his paws padding down the steps to the basement barely illuminated now by the throw of the flashlight. Silas followed him.

A rocking chair creaked. The woodstove flue tapped gently to the rustle of the wind outside. Snow tapped against the windowpanes. Bugsy growled, then sniffed the dank air below.

Silas strained to hear something moving, something whispering, something grasping the handle of an axe.

"Find anything?" Gustafson snapped as Silas and Bugsy burst back into the upstairs lodge bedroom.

"Naw, just some mice, I think. Must've been in this place all winter," Silas said.

"Or them ghosts again," said Gustafson.

Chapter XIII

The Greening of Noel McRae

A warm summer breeze whipped the grass against Noel McRae's boots. He drank in the subalpine scenery just east of Deadman's Lake. From the 4,300 foot elevation, he scanned the horizon south and peered down into the Green River Valley. He felt uneasy.

To the south, near Polar Star Mine, a pointy band of magnificent old-growth Douglas fir trees rose up from the lush valley floor. The ancient and distinctive forest marched in disorderly ranks seven miles down the banks of the Green River to Miners Creek near the borderline of the Gifford Pinchot National Forest far to the northwest.

He imagined himself an Indian, applying moccasin to mountainside to test his manhood, but discovering instead his oneness with nature.

His mind flitted about the terrain, its wholeness, its completeness, its utter silence. McRae's five senses merged into a singular sensation of the earth itself. City life, family fights, job tension, even world events in 1969 — all melted into a murky puddle of insignificance within the context of the wilderness that stretched out before him.

McRae earned his living as a speech therapist. With his wife Georgia and two sons, Robin and Jerry, McRae often ventured from their Longview home to hike the Cascades. Today, however, McRae had chosen to hike alone. He soaked in the solitude. Alone but not lonely, he tugged at his backpack shoulder straps. This should be relaxing, supremely relaxing. But for some reason, McRae's skin itched. He looked over his shoulder at the backcountry scenery. The hair prickled up on his neck.

He sighted in on a spaghetti network of logging roads and clearcuts snaking through the distant hills entering the pristine Green River Valley. Far beyond the lush valley, ugly hills, stubbled with slash and stumpy debris, heaved up from the surrounding forestland. Loggers had peeled back the skin of the earth, opening wounds that bled into the virgin Green River. McRae grimaced.

Fifty years earlier, the Green River Valley was typical of the old growth forests, stretching unbroken from the lowlands to the crest of the Cascade Range. Now the Green River timber stood vulnerable, an island in the middle of a disturbing sea of intensively managed state, private and federal tree farms.

McRae absorbed the view. He committed to memory the incredible ribbon of forestland lest Weyerhaeuser Co. or International Paper devour it. The feeling was emotional, perhaps even irrational, but he found it hard to shake. The evidence was all around him. Danger was a truck blowing up a cloud of dust on a logging road winding its way over the horizon towards the Green River Valley and Mount St. Helens to the south.

Something ought to be done. McRae pondered his dilemma. He was an ordinary guy unaccustomed to involvement in political issues. He preferred that government wage this battle for him. That's why he paid taxes, right?

He could have shrugged his shoulders and hiked home that day. Who would have blamed him? How should we use public land? The issue was then, as always, immense and imponderable. Who was Noel McRae to suggest a solution? Billions of board feet of timber were at stake. How dare he impose his views on the giant timber companies or the U.S. Forest Service or the hundreds of thousands of Northwest residents who depended on forest products for their livelihoods. After all, trees are a renewable resource! They grow back where they have been cut.

Nevertheless, Noel McRae feared that if he did not do something, the virgin forest of the Green River Valley might be clearcut before his boys had a chance to hike the trail with their own children some day.

McRae returned to his home and told Georgia about the eyeopening experience. Compelled to do something, he contacted the only conservation group he knew of. He wrote the president of the Sierra Club, saying in effect that something ought to be done.

The reaction of the club was predictably slow but not altogether surprising. The Sierra Club's northwest representative, Brock Evans, an attorney, replied that if something was to be done, then McRae would have to do it.

"We have found, time and again, that it is local people, getting actually, locally involved who can do the most good. If you think there is enough sentiment around Kelso and Longview to get something going in this area, then I think we can really work together and do something to save this area," Evans wrote back to McRae.

The friendliness of Evans' response encouraged McRae to proceed on his own. Evans' letter also broadened McRae's outlook. The more he dug into the issue of saving the Green River trail, the more McRae realized that what was needed was a plan enforced by the federal government to save all of the wilderness around Mount St. Helens.

Indeed, McRae quickly discovered that instead of 5,000 or 10,000 acres, he should be thinking in terms of 100,000 acres. His own particular concern for the Green River Valley was connected with other land use issues. Further south from where he had stood above the Green River Valley that summer day in 1969 was the 9,677-foot volcanic cone of Mount St. Helens. The snowcapped mountain loomed above a 1,262-acre body of water called Spirit Lake. These areas should be saved, too.

What furrowed McRae's brow most were the statistics describing man's use of the St. Helens environment. More than 150,000 people would visit Spirit Lake in search of the wilderness experience in 1970. Thirty-two years earlier, in 1938, only 17,000 people visited Spirit Lake. Despite the 900 percent increase in the number of hikers and campers, fishermen and hunters the past three decades, very little had been done to protect the environment from the increased use. Offroad vehicles, especially trail bikes, were gaining popularity in roadless areas. Motorboats towing skiers were commonplace on Spirit Lake. The public campgrounds on the south end of the lake routinely spilled over into unimproved areas.

The lodges and camps dotting the lake had not been enlarged during those growth years to accommodate the increasing numbers either. The tourist season was short, June through August, really. So why should an entrepreneur risk a lot of money with little expectation of a return?

The Forest Service contemplated tripling the size of the campground and would eventually put forth such a plan. That would put new pressure on the environment and also reduce the solitude that many sought in their trek to Mount St. Helens. McRae's head buzzed with the complexity of the public policy problem. Whenever the problem seemed insoluble, McRae would remember that the wilderness experience is not being "first" on the mountaintop, it is being "alone" on that remote precipice.

There also was constant talk of new commercial development in the region. Abandoned mines in the area attested to the lure of copper, silver and gold, the veins of which always seemed just beyond the reach of miners in the region the past 100 years. McRae winced at the idea of miners punching the Polar Star Mine into the flesh of the Green River Valley. Man is part of the wilderness, like the deer and the trees. The difference is that only man knows what is going on. Only man knows what is wilderness, and what was. Man is the earth's awareness of itself.

Finally, there were the summer camps dotting the Spirit Lake shoreline for McRae to consider. Since 1909, organized groups of children had been spending their summers at Spirit Lake, proving their mettle on the Mount Margaret backcountry trails. They numbered in the dozens back in 1913, back when campers had to hike three days to reach the original Portland YMCA camp on the south side of Spirit Lake. The summer campers numbered in the hundreds in 1927 when Lige Coalman, Fred Bradley and Louis Umiker built Holmstedt Memorial Lodge on the other side of the lake. Now, in 1969, literally thousands of boys and girls were pouring in from the lowland cities every summer to attend not only the Portland Y camp but also those camps operated by various other YMCA groups, the Boy Scouts, the Girl Scouts, the Episcopal church and other organizations.

There were ordinary business pressures to be considered in public policy discussions as well. Much of the land surrounding the Gifford Pinchot National Forest was owned by Weyerhaeuser Co. and Burlington Northern Railroad, not the U.S. Forest Service. These tree farms contained millions of dollars worth of timber planted and managed for the express purpose of being harvested. Burlington Northern had a longterm sales contract with International Paper that assured continued harvesting of timber within the same basin areas where the increasing numbers of recreational users would be hiking and camping, hunting and fishing.

McRae scratched his head in thought as he pondered the gauntlet thrown down by Sierra Club attorney Brock Evans. Multiple use of the forest seemed right. Certainly, trees are a renewable resource. The proof was all around him in well-managed, orderly, private tree farms. But should not certain areas be left alone, perpetually, so that people seeking a wilderness experience could feel the sky swoop down on them in the middle of the wild nowhere? McRae knew the answer and quickly befriended other conservationists who might help him in his effort.

At the recommendation of the Sierra Club, McRae contacted Dr. Russ L. Jolley in Portland, a man like McRae who found time outside his work to champion environmental causes.

Their first task was to identify specific issues connected with preservation of the Green River Valley. In 1970, they plotted strategy and educated themselves about other people's efforts to protect Mount St. Helens and the surrounding area.

In late 1970, McRae and Dr. Jolley learned that the Forest Service intended to sell timber in a small lake region just a mile off the Green River Trail. The Forest Service's impending Ghost Lake sale was four miles northeast of Spirit Lake. If logging roads were built and the trees in that area harvested, the pumiceous soil, especially at the 4,000-foot level, might not support reforestation. Also, the influx of dirtbikers and four-wheel drive enthusiasts would likely destroy the roads and trails in the region, not to mention the pristine quality of the high lakes.

What was really needed, reasoned McRae, was rehabilitation of the footpaths to the remote lakes from the youth camps along Spirit Lake. Forget logging. Open the region to the limited use by hikers to preserve the fragile environment of the Strawberry Lake and Ghost Lake areas. Preserve the wilderness by opening it to a trickle of foot traffic.

Jolley expressed the environmentalists' concerns this way in a January 23, 1971 letter to Ranger Harold W. Coates of the U.S. Forest Service:

"The most important fact to be considered is that recreation needs in the Spirit Lake area are . . . undeniable and the public demand for recreation is not restricted to the St. Helens side of the district boundary. There is not only the demand of the general public but also from the youth camps on the north side of Spirit Lake. For years, these camps have been able to give young people, mostly city kids from the Portland area, a fine backcountry experience, including pack trips along the Green River and to lakes north and east of the Green River.

"Two factors, overcrowding of the immediate Mount Margaret area and encroachment by roads and logging, have already contributed to a decline in the quality of this backcountry experience.

"Nearby logging roads . . . would . . . bring overuse to these relatively small lakes. In short, I believe the Ghost Sale is not in the public interest."

McRae took a similar approach in his own letter to the Randle District Ranger to restrict logging in the Upper Green River. Neither he nor Jolley, nor the Sierra Club for that matter, got much response to their appeal.

Four months later, McRae was counseled by the Sierra Club's Evans that his "nice guy" approach was not working.

"They only respond when you are tough with them. They want to log every place that has trees; it's as simple as that," Evans told McRae.

Though McRae was not yet ready to cave in to rampant cynicism, he hardened himself for a longterm battle. Saving the Green River Valley apparently meant saving Ghost Lake and Strawberry Lake. And saving those lakes meant tackling the Forest Service's timber sale plans for the Gifford Pinchot National Forest.

A reader and a thinker, McRae bored into the larger regional issues involved and found that others feeling as he did had suggested creation of a Mount St. Helens National Monument. There were, after all, other points of public interest worth preserving. The conservation effort must be, literally, monumental, sweeping, all-inclusive.

McRae's public policy position should include scenic points all around the mountain, including Indian pits, campgrounds, mineral springs and huckleberry fields, all open to the public. The best known of the springs was Iron Mike. The succulent berries in the area were, of course, legendary.

On the south side of Mount St. Helens, there were 15,000 acres of basalt lava beds with an extensive maze of subsurface lava tubes formed 1,900 years ago. McRae was not a cave explorer, but he knew of them on the east side of the Cowlitz-Skamania county line, between the southern timber line of Mount St. Helens and the Lewis River Canyon. The longest and best known was Ape Cave, some two miles long and 30 feet high. Other caves included Bat, Lake, Little Red River, and Spring, as well as Ole's Cave, named for a long-dead hermit, Ole Peterson. The big-eared Townsend's bats, Larch Mountain Salamanders and rare invertebrate species thrived in the dank, underground caves. The environments of lava tubes could certainly be permanently disrupted without federal protection.

McRae nursed along the idea of federal protection for the virgin timber, the lakes, the lava tubes and the mountain itself. Gradually, the idea of a national monument began to jell. He would be the catalyst for a movement of conservation groups. He pondered the "get tough" advice of Sierra Club attorney Brock Evans but continued in his own way to try to persuade the Forest Service to abandon its plan for the Ghost Lake timber sale and to be on guard for the preservation of the wilds.

On August 2, 1971, the Gifford Pinchot National Forest Supervisor Ross W. Williams formally announced his plan to go forward with the Ghost Sale.

McRae fought back, becoming an ad hoc leader of local environmentalists. In a Chehalis area home one evening, McRae, Evans and others decided to form the Mount St. Helens Protective Association.

Charles W. Dolan, conservation chairman of the Puget Sound Group of the Sierra Club, was delighted to hear of the Longview speech therapist's decision and wrote him a congratulatory letter August 4, 1971, two days after the Ghost Lake Sale decision:

"Dave Howard has informed me that you have been selected, appointed or volunteered to be the coordinator for the Mount St. Helens National Monument proposal." He went on to offer his advice and a wider base of support.

McRae began working with the Puget Sound chapter, especially Bob Werner of Chehalis, who was acting as subcommittee chairman for the group and the first chairman of the protective association. Other issues began to bubble to the surface, other timber sales, other conservation causes, some technical, some legal. It was a bit overwhelming. After all, McRae's main qualification was that he liked to hike.

On October 12, 1971, the Gifford Pinchot National Forest Supervisor Williams slightly revised his sale plan procedure but proceeded with the sale anyway. McRae and the Sierra Club members persisted in their opposition. On February 24, 1972, Sierra Club attorney Evans filed an appeal with Regional Forester Rexford A. Resler. It was too late, though, to meet the 60-day filing requirements and was dismissed. McRae, Evans, Russ Jolley, Bob Werner and others debated their next move.

In August, 1972, three years after Noel McRae's solo hike to Deadman's Lake, the environmentalists notified T. A. Schlapfer, the regional forester for Region VI of the U.S. Forest Service, of their intention to go to court and litigate the Ghost Sale. McRae could not figure out why the Forest Service had dug in its heels on the relatively small Ghost Sale issue, but he and others with him decided the area was too valuable to write off. The volcanic soil was too fragile to withstand road activity and logging, especially at the higher elevations. Certainly, most Spirit Lake people were more interested in the outstanding scenic resources than the paltry sum that the Forest Service might realize from a timber sale. And there seemed to be room within the Forest Service's regulations for multiple use of timberland to allow for a roadless area in the Green River Trail area to Ghost Lake.

On January 12, 1973, McRae and the environmentalists obtained a formal hearing of their appeal before Regional Forester T.A. Schlapfer. The Ghost Sale was stopped.

"They never built the road. There were a lot of times later when things would die down. When the Forest Service would start to make a move, we would leap to arms and stop it," recalled McRae of the Ghost Lake Sale battle.

Following up on their Ghost Lake Sale success, the environmentalists under the banner of the Columbia Group, Pacific Northwest Chapter of the Sierra Club in Portland, Oregon, made formal recommendations to the Forest Service for managing the Green River area as a roadless preserve, a wilderness for hikers and backpackers. The recommendations, submitted to Forest

Service Supervisor Ross W. Williams on March 3, 1973, pleaded for preservation of the area:

"The Green River Trail, an important resource, should be kept open and be maintained in its entirety, from Meta Lake to the Forest boundary. New trails could also be constructed... to provide an improved system of loop trails involving the Green River Valley and the high country on both sides.

"For many years, the existing trail system has been used for extended trail trips, especially by young people based at Spirit Lake. The recreational use of this entire area is, of course, increasing, and it should be borne in mind that these people do not come to see logging roads and clearcuts, but to travel the trails, camp along the river, view the lovely forested mountainsides, seek out remote lakes, and perhaps come upon a herd of elk along the Green River as a Sierra Club group did last fall, 1972."

Concurrent with the Ghost Lake Sale issue, environmentalists literally stumbled across a logging road built in the fall of 1974 by Weyerhaeuser Co. across two sections of Forest Service timberland to reach their property. Doug Scott, a Sierra Club representative, called the three-mile road along Miners Creek "one of the most deceitful things the Forest Service has ever allowed to happen in this area." Mervin F. Wolf, a spokesman for the Gifford Pinchot National Forest recreational staff, denied the charges:

"A permit was issued to the Weyerhaeuser Co. over a year ago (1973)... to reach their property. They did what they were legally entitled to do—they have the right of ingress and egress. But we are embarrassed at not knowing the road had been built. There was certainly no attempt to deceive anyone, and we told the environmental groups about it as soon as we found out ourselves."

The environmentalists broadened their base of support, attracting the Friends of the Earth and mainstream politicians, chief among them Congressman Don Bonker. Miners Creek became a rallying cry.

Before spring thaw filled Miners Creek with snow melt, Noel McRae and the environmentalists had another victory with a 29,000-acre land exchange agreement between Weyerhaeuser and the Forest Service in which the company gave 540 crucial wilderness acres to the Forest Service and agreed to drop efforts to acquire 800 other acres of timberland that environmentalists felt could be better used for recreation.

McRae lost some battles, too, mainly from inattention, such as the road into a timber sale next to Strawberry Lake.

"Most of the time we were lucky to feel like we were treading water," he said.

The land exchange between the Forest Service and Weyerhaeuser seemed to preserve the low elevation forest near Mount St. Helens. The land exchange saved the 500- and 600-year-old trees along with the important trail access to the Mount Margaret backcountry as well as the salmon spawning ground in the Green River. Noel McRae had reason to smile, but the everpresent "multiple use" designation by the Forest Service of so much of the surrounding roadless areas clouded the victory.

The Sierra Club, Friends of the Earth and the Mount St. Helens Protective Association had fought six years to save Miners Creek and nearby lands on the Green River. An inescapable paradox confronted McRae and his group: The outrage felt by the environmentalists towards the Forest Service for having "deceived" them about the secretly constructed road, turned out to have focused public opinion on the area. The public attention prompted Third District Representative Don Bonker to get involved. The snowballing furor also prompted Ted Schlapfer, regional forester for the Forest Service, to personally handle the negotiation of the land exchange with Weyerhaeuser. Perhaps Brock Evans' advice to McRae was right after all: "They only respond when you are tough with them." Perhaps, too, a continued toughminded approach might result in creation of a national monument that would take in all 85,000, or more, acres of lava tubes, virgin forests, wilderness lakes and Mount St. Helens itself. McRae pondered the possibility.

The idea of a national monument was not original with McRae and Jolley. For 50 years there had been talk of the Forest Service swapping back to the federal government the extensive land holdings granted to the Northern Pacific Railroad in 1864 to assist it in building its transcontinental line. The railroad, which became Burlington Northern, owned a checkerboard of sections comprising half of the land in the greater Mount St. Helens area, including the pinnacle.

McRae researched the issue and incorporated into his own thinking the ideas of others. They included Dr. William Halliday who in the December, 1963, issue of *National Parks Magazine* recommended creation of a national monument to guarantee protection of the extensive system of lava tubes and the volcanic tree castings around Mount St. Helens. Philip R. Pryde took up the cause in that same magazine in May, 1968, with his argument for a monument entitled "Mount Saint Helens: A Possible National Monument."

Conservationists over the years had directed their efforts towards saving individual areas that made St. Helens special. McRae and his group, with the Miners Creek success, for instance, had limited their fight to that portion of the Mount Margaret backcountry. However, logging still threatened the Green River Valley and remote high lakes area. And there were still the lava caves, Spirit Lake and finally the scenic mountain itself. Thus, McRae became convinced that his efforts should be directed towards creation of an all-inclusive monument. It would be a long, complicated, unpaid fight in which it would be difficult for McRae not to cave in to the "us-them" antagonism of so many other Sierra Club environmentalists. He sought cooperation, despite the onset of new threats to the backcountry and Spirit Lake, not just from logging, but also renewed mining interests.

In 1976, Eli Smith presented his plan for opening the old Sweden (Coe's) Mine in pursuit of copper and other minerals, possibly gold and silver. The Forest Service owned the surface rights while Smith's Mount St. Helens Mining Company had a deed to the land's mineral and mining improvements. Smith asked and was granted Forest Service permission to clear an area for a helicopter landing pad in the wilderness area. He was also given permission to tunnel further in Sweden Mine and place waste material in the vicinity of the entrance.

Environmentalists were outraged. YMCA and other summer youth camp officials grew concerned. Panicky phone calls poured in to the Forest Service offices. The various lodge operators around Spirit Lake squirmed at the prospects.·

Also, a new voice sang out in defense of the mountain. It belonged to Susan Saul, a woman new to the Kelso-Longview area. She quickly deduced that the mining activity would surely result in construction of a road into the roadless area from Independence Pass. She hiked into the mining site near Spirit Lake one warm July Sunday in 1976. Arriving before noon, she asked the miners what they were doing. Coe Creek near the mine entrance was muddy from brown spoils being dumped by the miners.

"Workers were present at the site and a man, who identified himself as the head of the on-site mining operations, said that they were in the process of clearing a mud slide about 500 feet inside the tunnel."

Longview's *Daily News* railed editorially on August 18, 1976, that mining was incompatible with recreation in the Spirit Lake area:

"You can hear the motor driving the air compressor at the old Coe's Mine site nearly a mile away. As you pass the Portland YMCA camp at the north end of Spirit Lake, the noise grows louder.

"Then you see the creek. The water seems clear enough, but the bottom is an orangish rust color sediment from the seepage from the mine, which runs at a steady flow from the mine mouth. The sediment covers the rocks and creek bottom in all but the swiftest flowing portions of the stream. You can even find it at the creek's mouth where it empties into the lake.

"At the mine mouth, men have hastily dug a pit next to the shaft. The seepage is supposed to flow into it, settle, and then flow into the creek.

"Pipe and other debris from earlier mining ventures is strewn about. A mining railroad runs into the shaft which the men working it say has been cleared back 1,000 feet or more.

"What comes out of the mine gets dumped — along the old tailings deposits or along the creek bank.

"This commercial operation is set in a tract of virgin forest in a recreation area which is enjoyed by tens of thousands of persons each year.

"Quite clearly, it does not belong."

Soon, for a variety of governmental and economic reasons, mining activity along Coe Creek stopped. Governmental red tape ensnarled Smith and his mining efforts. But the most important result of the controversy was the alliance of Saul with McRae as co-chairpersons of the soon-to-be-revitalized Mount St. Helens Protective Association. Saul would be crucial in the effort.

As quickly as the mining issue faded, the logging issue re-emerged. This time, the threat of logging brought the creation of a national monument into sharp focus. In February, 1977, Oregonians and Washingtonians, led by McRae and Saul, among others, re-established the Mount St. Helens Protective Association. McRae did not feel the Forest Service was guarding this scenic wilderness area. Thus to combat mining and logging interests, the association wanted to create a special protected status for St. Helens. The new association created its own newspaper, the *Monument News,* to fuel the campaign.

The issue to save St. Helens became one of numbers. Everybody — loggers, miners, hikers, climbers, fishermen and hunters, and the Forest Service — agreed some portion of the mountain should be protected as wilderness. How much, was the issue. The U.S. Forest Service was caught in the middle of the debate.

The issue affected jobs in the region. Entrepreneurs in the area had risked hundreds of thousands of dollars on mills that required log supplies off public lands. Indirect employment in the forest products industry numbered in the hundreds of thousands. Without private sector risk-takers willing to gamble their capital and their time on sawmills and plywood plants, there would be no buyers for any of the billions of board feet of public timber, thus rendering the asset economically worthless. The government, therefore, needed industry to bid on public timber and give it monetary value.

Also, aside from the contemplative value to a very few hearty outdoorsmen, an old growth wilderness in a remote part of the United States does not directly benefit the citizenry who own the national forestland unless and until the timber is sold. If not sold, timber in a wilderness eventually dies and rots, again, a waste to the vast majority of the people who own it.

On the other hand, the timberline logging and the ugly lacework of eroded roads on Mount St. Helens clearly demonstrated to environmentalists how national forests should not be managed. They argued that the Forest Service could not be trusted with protection of the wilderness domain, which in itself was of national value.

The Forest Service squirmed in discomfort with the irresolvable wilderness issue. Wilderness areas, after all, are a luxury item. They are available to the public because we as a nation are willing to set aside tracts of economically valuable resources for people to "experience," and little more. How much wilderness we as a society can afford was, and is, the heart of the public policy issue.

By midyear, 1978, McRae and the environmentalists found their arguments for creating a preserve gaining wider acceptance. *The Daily News* in Longview invited its readers to write letters answering the question, "Do you believe roads and logging should be permitted in those areas, or should they be kept as they are for recreational use?" The newspaper had its greatest response ever to a Reader Forum, published June 28, 1978, with 60 letters crying out in near unanimity in their opposition to all logging on St. Helens. Typical of the Reader Forum responses were the following:

Truckdriver Earle E. Miller could not see the value of clearcutting St. Helens only to export the logs to Japan. "It appears the almighty dollar has become our god."

Grocery store owner Lena A. Withers said yes to roads, no to logging. "I think the major lumber industries have enough land for logging."

Carpenter Kyle M. Ward recalled that his great-grandfather Joseph Burgoyne homesteaded in the heartbreakingly beautiful Buckhorn Basin behind the base of Mount Margaret. "If we let people like George Weyerhaeuser totally devastate this land, we are defeating ourselves. We are slowly destroying our environment and wildlife so that our future children will have nothing."

Retiree Walter A. Wooton urged preservation of the mountain to which he drove in 1923 over rough forest trails to the edge of Spirit Lake. "Next morning at daylight, we hiked to the mountain and on to the top."

Weyerhaeuser Co. woods security man Mark Gilchrist called for preservation of the Gifford Pinchot for recreation and wildlife. "Please, don't allow any camping and hiking area to become polluted by noisy log trucks and scarred by clearcut land."

Finally, retired carpenter and millwright Harold Cornwell summed up the feelings of many. "My family and I are 100 percent against any roads built around Spirit Lake and Mount St. Helens. I have lived in the Kelso area since

1925, and have backpacked and packed by horses all the trails north, south, east and west of Spirit Lake. The log roads have destroyed nearly all of them. Save all the country around and back of Spirit Lake for recreation and wild game. It's a dirty shame to see nothing but stumps and log roads in that beautiful country."

There was a quiet ripple of embarrassment within the editorial pages of *The Daily News* for the emotional and rather sensational response to what should have been a debatable issue. The volume and lopsidedness of the response fueled the efforts of environmentalists against the private timber companies and the Forest Service. The newspaper castigated its own readers for their shallow understanding of industrial forestry and the efforts of forest management of the Forest Service and the timber companies.

The Daily News' editorial raked its readers this way:

"That's beautiful country, and we too believe it should remain unspoiled. However, it is discouraging to read between the lines of the Reader Forum responses and realize that many people in Cowlitz County have no more understanding of what forests are all about than those in New Jersy do.

"People here are apparently also unfamiliar with the accomplishments of the Forest Service and industrial foresters. Let us say right now that private, industrial foresters (and Weyerhaeuser is a leader) are taking better care of their forests than the United States of America is."

While public issues were not, and are not, settled in the Reader's Forum of *The Daily News*, the Forest Service began to feel the heat of public opinion, and it was only beginning. Four generations of Northwest residents had attended the youth camps and stayed in the Spirit Lake lodges since the beginning of the 20th Century. The opinions of these thousands of people began to filter down to their elected representatives in Congress. They wanted the coming generations of the 21st Century to enjoy Mount St. Helens, too.

The Mount St. Helens issue gradually became part of a much larger, national wilderness issue that would be known as RARE II. In August, 1978, a coalition of 23 different environmental groups proposed that wilderness areas be increased to 2.1 million acres in Washington and another 3 million acres in Oregon. All the roadless areas in the Mount St. Helens—Spirit Lake region were included. The Mount St. Helens wilderness status for 91,230 acres would apply to the mountain itself, Mount Margaret backcountry, the roadless portion of Green River Valley, the Strawberry Mountain area and a small roadless area south of St. Helens known as Kipuka.

The stage was set now for the Forest Service to sift through its public commentary and write recommendations for Congress to consider in 1979.

Loggers with truck payments and mill owners with mortgages planned their business operations with no idea how much public timber the Forest Service would put out to bid on in the coming years. Timber operators and lumber manufacturers chafed at the arguments made by the Sierra Club preservationists who they felt had nothing personally at risk in their struggle to achieve wilderness status for public timberlands. The businessmen, on the other hand, felt they risked everything in the debate. The irony, from their point of view, was that without them taking risks, employing people, sawing lumber and fueling the national economy, the nation would not even be able to afford to set aside timberlands for wilderness designation.

Forest Service officials were nervous about appearing fair and even-handed and actively sought public "panel" recommendations for land use planning of national forests. Congressmen and governors in both Oregon and Washington were sweating re-election. RARE II—Roadless Area Review and Evaluation—became the battle cry for what was shaping up to be one of the hottest environmental issues of the 1980s.

In the middle of the fray was one Noel McRae. Ten years earlier, he never dreamed his interest in keeping logging roads out of the Green River Valley would lead to this. McRae was just one man, but he inspired a cadre of seasoned environmentalists, including Susan Saul, who was chief among the workers and perhaps the most dedicated organizer in the association. Savvy in affairs political, she knew her way to Representative Don Bonker's office and she could, when necessary, grind out a press release off the top of her head from a phone booth.

On January 4, 1979, U.S. Department of Agriculture Secretary Bob Berglund announced the completion of the RARE II study. The scope of the study was national and called for doubling of the nation's protected wilderness by adding 15.1 million acres of public forest land, mainly in Alaska.

Mount St. Helens was not included among the lands classified as wilderness. Instead, Secretary Berglund said further planning was needed for Mount Margaret, 22,076 acres; Mount St. Helens, 25,680 acres; and Kipuka, 5,030 acres. The remaining 22,703 acres in the Mount Margaret area, as well as the entire 7,230-acre Strawberry Mountain area to the east was designated "multiple use," meaning open to logging, mining and recreation. The environmentalists were stunned.

Joe Walicki of the Wilderness Society's Northwest Regional Office in Portland said, "The Forest Service has not kept their promise and we feel cheated. We plan to take the fight to the halls of Congress."

The Sierra Club, the National Audubon Society and Friends of the Earth joined the Wilderness Society in expressing "acute disappointment." Noel McRae and Susan Saul commiserated with one another and their fellow members of the Mount St. Helens Protective Association. RARE II did not achieve their goals. The environmentalists felt that none of the recreational areas around Mount St. Helens would be safe without a wilderness designation. They felt the lava tubes, virgin forests, pristine lakes, fragile alpine meadows and the snowy volcanic peak itself, would all go unprotected from possible mining and logging, geothermal development and motor vehicle traffic.

The suspicion among the environmentalists was that the govenment's strategy was to defuse opposition to mining and logging by delaying a decision on Mount St. Helens' status.

As for McRae's beloved Green River Valley, RARE II relegated it to "further study." In 10 years, what had he accomplished? A holding action? McRae realized the Forest Service was never going to preserve the Mount Margaret backcountry, especially the low elevation, old-growth timber in the Green River Valley. It would take an act by Congress to achieve the vision he had had for the Green River Valley that summery day in 1969. Wilderness use was increasing 8 percent annually since 1969. McRae could not understand how anybody in business, government or the community at large failed to see a need for more, not less, wilderness. McRae and the band of individuals loosely united under the protective association banner would not disappear though. The government would have to put up with them a while longer.

In December, 1979, Washington Congressman Tom Foley introduced a bill for the National Forest Multiple-Use Management Act. The bill would permanently exclude from wilderness designation all "nonwilderness" roadless areas under RARE II. Mount St. Helens, the Green River area and the Mount Margaret backcountry and the lava tubes south of the volcano would never attain wilderness status under the bill.

The battle in Congress loomed ahead. On February 24, 1980, Ken Gersten, western Washington coordinator for the Washington Wilderness Coaltion, urged McRae, Susan Saul and Russ Jolley to prepare for the coming battle. Gersten tucked this advice in an envelope to the protective association members:

"Keep getting psyched. Get your newsletter going again . . . If you don't already have a letterhead and logo, you should consider designing them. . . You might want to incorporate . . . It protects people in the organization from legal action . . . Work on increasing your membership and treasury . . . Bake sales, garage sales, buttons and T-shirts are all good fundraisers . . .

"The more you know about Mount St. Helens and Mount Margaret, the easier it will be to answer questions and to argue effectively with the timber beasts . . . Keep training your people . . . Have periodic field trips so your new people get on-the-ground training ... The field trips will also keep you and everyone else going when things seem slow ... Mix in some potlucks and retreats as well."

Gersten's suggestion of a "field trip" seemed a fitting way to bring the protective association members back together again in the spring of 1980. The Green River Valley trail with its relic, old-growth Douglas fir canopy likewise seemed a fitting destination. Noel McRae would lead the group. Susan Saul would publicize the hike in the *Monument News* and *The Daily News*. She got the Willapa Hills Audubon Society and the Mount St. Helens Hiking Club to cosponsor the hike and worked out the details of carpooling from the Longview Public Library to the trailhead.

The date set for the Green River hike was May 10, 1980.

There would be plenty of time on the hike to formulate political strategy for the coming fray in Congress to create a 176,000-acre Mount St. Helens National Scenic Area. More than half of the area would be proposed for wilderness designation. Saul figured that, surrounded by firs half a millenium old, few people on a protection association hike up the Green River would argue against wilderness designation for the 91,000 acres of Kipuka, Mount St. Helens, Mount Margaret and the Strawberry Mountain areas within the proposed scenic area.

Suddenly, though, two months before the hike, the public's attention was diverted on March 27, 1980, when Mount St. Helens—the volcano!—awakened.

Portland radio station KGW broadcast the first visual sighting of smoke and ash spewing forth from a small crater on the pinnacle. The media turned Harry Truman's lodge into a stage. The television networks turned their kleig lights on the scientists of the U.S. Geological Survey at a makeshift press center in Vancouver, Washington. The issue of man preserving the wilderness from other men suddenly seemed a little ridiculous. McRae and Saul considered postponing the hike.

To the superstitious residents around the suddenly active volcano, the rumblings were a matter of mythology. There was a common feeling that "The Lady" had had enough of the logging, camping, mining, hiking, and everything else connected with the white man's adventures around St. Helens since the volcano erupted 123 years earlier.

To scientists, the sudden rumblings of the mountain came as no surprise. Indeed the U.S. Geological Survey had predicted activity in the near future only a few years earlier.

To the ordinary person familiar with the Cascade Range, the renewed volcanic activity came as no real surprise either. A young mountain, newly emerged from the sea, Mount St. Helens was located west of the the Cascade crest only 2,000 feet above sea level. It had the lowest timberline of any mountain in the state. Elsewhere in the Cascade Range, the timberline is typically at the 6,600 foot level. Cinder and pumice from eruptions as recent as the early and mid-1800s still choked off in 1980 the advance of lodgepole pine forests at the 4,200 foot level.

To Noel McRae, Susan Saul, Russ Jolley and all the other environmentalists, the eruptive behavior of Mount St. Helens in March and subsequently that April, 1980, threatened to distract the protective association from obtaining monument status for the area. What to do?

County sheriff's deputies closed off roads leading into the Red Zone areas closest to the mountain, but Weyerhaeuser Co. continued to send loggers into its lands adjacent to the Gifford Pinchot National Forest. And, life was continuing around Mount St. Helens. Indeed, lodge owner Harry Truman and sundry others dared the mountain to erupt. So why not continue the efforts of the Mount St. Helens Protective Association?

Saul and McRae decided the May 10 hike up the Green River Trail was "on."

On the day of the hike, the mountain was quiet. Nobody suspected St. Helens would erupt in all its fury eight days later. No. Today, Saturday, May 10, was to be a day of spiritual rejuvenation for the protective association. And it was for some members, but not all.

Early that Saturday morning, about 7:30 or so, retiree Harold Deery stirred restlessly in anticipation of the hike. The Green River Trail was clear of snow and open for the season. The views would be spectacular. But the rumblings of the volcano had been frequent and unpredictable the past two months. He was nervous.

As people arrived at the Longview Library, talk centered around the mountain. Harry Truman was in all the newspapers. People were moving belongings out of their cabins and lodges. The worldwide attention focused on the mountain the past two months had been exciting, but there was little in the newspapers to alarm McRae and Saul. So the hikers left for St. Helens that morning, despite Harold Deery's eerie premonition.

Deery and his wife Ruth, Hermine Soler, Sarah Detherage, Jim Fletcher, Arlene Walker, Russ Jolley, Jean Lancaster, Russ Maynard, Mary Ellen Covert and two dozen others drove to Castle Rock, then up Spirit Lake Highway to the Mount St. Helens Loop Road. There, they hooked up with Weyerhaeuser Logging Road 2500 and drove to the Green River Valley trailhead southwest of Miners Creek. Just inside the western boundary of the Gifford Pinchot National Forest on the Lewis-Skamania county line, the hikers parked their vehicles. Donning wool hats and rain parkas, they headed out towards the old, abandoned guard station and hiked up Trail 213 — the Green River Valley Trail.

The temperature hovered in the low 50s. Amid the "ooohs" and "aaahs," Saul would tell hikers what they could do to preserve the old-growth forest that gradually enveloped them. In these woods, time had a way of grinding to a slow tick. The trail followed the rushing Green River. None of the uphill climbs were strenuous, but the group of hikers gradually broke apart into five or six hiking units. McRae worried about stragglers but kept up his pace.

Pale green moss gave way to deep, green deer clover. An elk hunter's shack appeared. McRae had complained in the past about the shack at the first horse ford on the Green River. The roof, made of 22 strips of sheet metal, was falling down. Strewn everywhere were remnants of Coleman fuel cans, dirty dishes, stainless steel silverware, empty liquor bottles, crushed beer cans, an empty food cache, plastic caps, plastic tops, plastic bottles, plastic food wrappers and plastic knives, forks and spoons, detritus of an arrogant, wasteful civilization.

Botanically minded stragglers pondered the devil's club near the water's edge. McRae from time to time rounded up the group and pressed ahead. Harold Deery meanwhile fretted nervously even though he was 13 air miles north of the volcano in a protected drainage that had three mountains all more than 5,000 feet high to shield him from an eruption. Finally, he could stand it no longer. Deery halted before lunch and walked back to the parking lot where he sweated out the remainder of the day until everybody else returned.

Eight days later, Mount St. Helens erupted. The blast that Sunday morning eruption at 8:32 a.m. would have killed Harold Deery in his car parked at the Green River trailhead.

McRae and the association membership were stunned by the devastation of May 18. They pondered whether the Mount St. Helens Protective Association even had a cause to champion now that the blast had lowered the mountain 1,300 feet. Hundreds of thousands of animals were dead. The lateral blast flattened vast grid squares of timber. In their lifetime, none of the protective association members could expect to see the return of the mountain and Spirit Lake to its original state of beauty.

Depressed by dozens of people's deaths and a steady stream of ashen gray pictures of ancient firs flattened in an area eight miles by fifteen miles, many of the most determined environmentalists dropped out of the movement.

Ironically, the Green River Valley survived. The steepness of the valley walls and the mountain barrier between it and St. Helens had spared the timber along the Green River from the fate of the surrounding forestland. McRae sensed a great loss from the blast but he also began feeling a need, more than ever before, to preserve the Green River Valley and the surrounding blast zone of Mount St. Helens as a national monument.

On June 5, 1980, the protective association met at Harold Deery's home in Longview to discuss the just-introduced volcanic monument bill of Kansas Republican Representative Keith Sebelius. Jim Blomquist and Charlie Raines of the Sierra Club and Ken Gersten of the Wilderness Coalition joined them, offering the continued support of their organizations. There was much to talk about. The lava tubes on the south side of the mountain were untouched by the blast. Kipuka was intact. And the narrow band of virgin timber in the Green River Valley, surrounded by high mountains and sequestered in a steep gorge, had survived. The blast had blown right over the top of the valley.

Determined to go on in their work, Susan Saul proposed increasing the size of the proposed monument to 216,000 acres, far exceeding the scope of two proposals put forth by the association the past 10 years. Roadless areas had been increased "naturally" by the eruption which added 25,000 acres to the the approximately 95,000 acres previously designated that way by the Forest Service's RARE II plan several years earlier.

For several months there was some disarray among the remaining environmentalists. The issues were different now. Salvage logging was underway, but so was silt removal from clogged rivers. Spirit Lake was relocated by the blast and threatened to flood the valleys below unless the Army Corps of Engineers could somehow drain it. Saul and McRae re-evaluated their previous monument proposals and decided that monument status was appropriate more than ever. Nowhere in the continental United States, they felt, was there a site more deserving of wilderness status.

The association, co-chaired by McRae and Saul, officially proposed January 15, 1981, creation of the monument with endorsements of the Sierra Club, National Audubon Society, Willapa Hills and Seattle Audubon Societies, Washington Wilderness Coalition, Washington Native Plant Society, Friends of the Earth, the Wilderness Society and the Washington Environmental Council.

Timber interests lined up in opposition to the environmentalists. They argued for a 40,000-acre monument, restricted to the blast zone only.

Eighteen months later, a compromise hailed by all sides was reached with President Reagan's signature on a bill creating a 110,000-acre preserve.

Politicians hailed the bill. Southwest Washington Democrat Don Bonker deserved most of the credit, but Senators Slade Gorton and Henry Jackson deserved kudos too. Susan Saul also achieved national recognition for her part when she won Gulf Oil's Conservation Award in 1983.

Newspaper accounts and television broadcasts noted repeatedly that approval of the bill creating a monument ended a "two-year" struggle over the future of Mount St. Helens. Noel McRae's 12-year struggle went unnoticed in the press and at the dedication of the monument at the U.S. Forest Service Visitors Center on May 18, 1983. The quiet, unassuming speech therapist, father of two now-grown sons, McRae smiled wanly at the irony of news accounts. His thoughts turned towards hiking with his wife Georgia up the Green River Valley trail, spared by the volcanic fury of Mother Nature and, now, preserved from the hand of industrial man.

Epilogue

Dispatches From The Red Zone

At 43 seconds past 3:47 p.m., Thursday, March 20, the first shock waves of an impending eruption resounded through the rock beneath St. Helens at 19,600 feet per second, tripping seismometers throughout the region. On the Richter scale, the quake measured 4.1.

University of Washington geophysicists Steve Malone and Craig Weaver figured it was "just an earthquake." But the jagged etches up and down the green-ruled graph paper of the seismograph persisted, indicating that tremor activity was increasing. They pinpointed the vortex of their excitement directly beneath Mount St. Helens.

Together with a third geophysicist, Elliot Endo, the scientists packed a vehicle with delicate sensing gear and headed south down Interstate 5 to a then little known recreational area called Spirit Lake. They rendezvoused with U.S. Forest Service personnel who helped them set up the seismic measuring gear.

St. Helens' shaking continued Friday and Saturday, March 21-22, and on through the weekend. Word of a possible eruption still seemed farfetched, yet we in the news media glommed on the story with a zeal matched only by that of volcanologists who foresaw a once-in-a-lifetime opportunity to study a volcano close up. At last, a volcanic laboratory within an easy commute of home.

By Monday, the mountain swarmed with brooding earthquakes and anxious scientists. News media cameramen strafed the precipice for telltale puffs of smoke. Nobody wanted to look silly by overreacting, but nobody wanted to miss one of nature's greatest wonders right in our own neighborhood, either.

On Tuesday, March 25, the top news story was the growing possibility of an eruption. There was no real basis for the speculation except for the increasing tremor activity. Small avalanches ripped across the face of St. Helens. Additional seismometers were installed to monitor the tremors and measure earth movement. The media, government and scientific community pondered the mountain's next move.

The problem was not a simple one. The media, government and the scientific community all had choices to make. The media could entertain, inform or alarm. Government could enact drastic safety measures. Yet, safety had its price, in terms of financial and personal hardship on the people living and working in the vicinity. Scientists were looked to as the ultimate arbiters on the issue, but they simply did not know much about the phenomenon. What to do?

On Wednesday, March 26, city, county, state and federal government officials met in Vancouver along with Weyerhaeuser and International Paper representatives to discuss closing some of the roads around the mountain. The committee would not reach an official "Red Zone" decision signed by Washington Governor Dixy Lee Ray until April 30.

Washington Emergency Services did, however, impose road closures as early as March 31 to protect sightseers from what was euphemistically referred to as "specific events." It would be logistically impossible to warn everybody within the closed areas of a volcanic eruption.

The debate over the seriousness of the eruption threat raged among news directors and reporters, photographers and newspaper editors. What do we have here? The mountain could erupt tomorrow. It could erupt 100 years from now. Should the volcano become a "beat" to cover the way we cover City Hall?

I was a reporter for the *Oregon Statesman* in Salem. I covered the eruption of Mount St. Helens as a mountain melodrama to be continued on the front page day after day. I viewed the early rumblings the way I viewed any car wreck: a tragedy today, forgotten tomorrow. From the initial venting of ash and steam in March, 1980, I helped script the soap opera, drawing heavily on the ingredients of any good potboiler: fear, doubt and uncertainty.

At the *Oregon Statesman*, one of my many bosses, news editor Don

Scarborough, anguished over placement of the story. Page 1? Above the fold? Below? Or the regional section front? Again, above or below the fold? Like editors at all news media — radio, television and newspapers — Scarborough sought to inform without unnecessarily alarming his readers.

As a writer looking for a byline, my approach was to milk the story for all it was worth. We haggled and fiddled until a compromise was reached between the hot-headed reporting staff and the cooler, more experienced editors who ran the newspaper. The debate continued, though, with daily scientific revelations fueling our arguments.

Mike Beard ended the debate over the seriousness of the eruptive behavior on Thursday, March 27. Normally, Beard provided air traffic reports for Portland radio station KGW. Today, though, he expanded his report to include the first significant volcanic sputterings.

"This thing's erupting! There's smoke and ashes pouring out of it. There is no doubt the eruption is starting. You can see the ash very, very clearly against the snow," Beard blurted into his microphone. From Bangkok to Paris, the news reverberated around the world.

I read Beard's report line by line as it clacked across the teletype into our newsroom in Salem, Oregon. Like most Northwesterners, I was familiar with the 9,677-foot peak, snowy and serene. My wife Cheryl and I could hardly escape noticing the graceful symmetry of St. Helens from the Banfield Freeway as we headed east out of Portland toward the yawning Columbia River Gorge to visit her folks near Gresham. And now Beard's report: I literally rubbed my eyes in disbelief.

Also, you could not miss Mount St. Helens' beauty on cloudless days en route between Seattle and Portland up Interstate 5. Even at sixty miles per hour, Mount St. Helens looked as delectable as a scoop of vanilla perched atop a sugar cone. Few freeway motorists thought "volcanic cone" until now, that is.

After KGW's Beard had made it official, my city editor, Dan Davies, hailed me and several other reporters for the news assignment we had been begging for.

"Your wish has come true. Head north," Davies said. Fellow staffer Daniel Postrel and I did not need much urging, seeing as how we were locked in bitter competition with the staff of the rival Salem daily, *The Capital Journal.*

The uncertainty of an eruption was the stuff of our news coverage. During those first few weeks. Weyerhaeuser Co. had 300 employees working logging sites in the area. Pulling the men out of the woods now might jeopardize the log supplies at its mills in the region. How long should it curtail logging? A week? A month? Until the mountain quit shaking? And how long would that be? Nobody knew. I learned to spin a news story out of such intangible uncertainty.

Thousands of people maintained permanent as well as recreational residences in the area. Should they pack out their belongings and start all over? Who would reimburse them for their loss? Nobody knew, and that again became the grist for news.

There were the small businessmen and -women who likewise felt the uncertainty. Don Platt's Lone Fir Resort in Cougar south of St. Helens was booming with the influx of volcano watchers. Dot Elmire at the Cougar general store had never seen anything like the business she was getting. On the opposite side of the mountain, Stanley Lee, proprietor of the Kid Valley Grocery fretted over evacuation or closure because it would wipe him out financially. He had invested $20,000 in the mid-1950s in his store and 10 acres and was hoping to sell out and retire as soon as the U.S. Forest Service finished tripling the size of tourist facilities at Spirit Lake. Their situations were typical. Their sense of uncertainty was collective, suddenly tangible, and strangely common.

The government felt the volcano posed a health hazard and closed the area where Lee Mattson lived. A grizzled carpenter and father of two small children, Mattson's blood simmered at the thought of the sheriff's department blocking the road to his cabin on the flanks of St. Helens for the rest of the spring and summer and who knew how long. His job, his family life, his residency in the Northwest had always been uncertain, but for reasons other than a potential eruption of a volcano. Perhaps the economy threatened his carpentry income. Other times snow prevented him from reaching his cabin. And there were a plethora of problems that isolate family members from one another. But rarely did uncertainty surrounding his life take the form of a shrewish, unpredictable volcano. He fumed.

Nervous officials from all levels of government began debating the issue. What to do? Washington Governor Dixy Lee Ray and her staff pondered the boundaries for an expanded "Red Zone." Too many Lee Mattson's would pose serious political problems.

Sheriff William Closner of Skamania County, where Harry Truman's lodge was located, pondered his own special problem with the 83-year-old mountain man who had made his home on the shore line of Spirit Lake the past 54 years. Truman's celebrity posed a serious challenge to law enforcement if the order for a closure came down from the state.

On March 30, Truman temporarily left his beloved St. Helens Lodge and allowed himself to be driven by a deputy sheriff to the Toutle Lake School. He stepped from the four-wheel and strode to the center of the excited assemblage of reporters and photographers from all over the world. The press conference at Toutle Lake School, far below the dangerous "Red Zone" around St. Helens was a stage for the wily entrepreneur. He did not disappoint us.

"Shoot me head on, boys. Don't shoot me from the side," he commanded the photographers grinding away from every angle.

"We had a show yesterday morning, boys. It rolled my bed clear across the room and I decided it was time to get up. It woke me up about five. It's a thrill, a strange sensation. I'd love it if I wasn't scared to death," he chortled. "The mountain's shot its wad, and it hasn't hurt my place a bit. But those goddamn geologists with hair down to their butts wouldn't pay no attention to ol' Truman. I don't think they know any more about the inside of that mountain than I do — and I don't know nothing about the inside of her."

But would he leave?

"You couldn't pull me out with a mule team. That mountain's part of Truman and Truman's part of that mountain," he said. On his way back to his lodge, he signed off with "OK, you buzzards, I'll see you in church."

To keep his mind off the quakes, Harry was obviously reassuring himself that the news media, the government and the U.S. Geological Survey would have choppers landing on top of each other to rescue him when and if the mountain actually blew up. Here at the school, Truman winked and waved his arms and bragged about his cache of Schenley's whiskey to get him through "anything." But among his relatives and closer friends, his story was more cautious, reserved, fearful.

"You know, I am scared as hell about earthquakes; I just wish it would stop all the shaking," he said, according to Shirley Rosen's recollection of her legendary uncle in *Truman of St. Helens.* She and others close to Harry knew the flipside version was that of a lonely, frightened old man who protected himself from the realization of his own smallness compared to the mountain by entertaining the NBC-TV Today Show crew. He poured Schenley's all around and put a few rolls of music on his antique player piano to forget the horror of clinking dishes and creaking timbers.

On April 2, St. Helens rocked with earthquakes measuring 4.5 and 4.7 on the Richter Scale.

On April 3, St. Helens Lodge shook from a new kind of seismic activity called a harmonic tremor. The mountain experienced a quake measuring 4.8. but unlike previous activity, the tremors persisted. Governor Ray declared a state of emergency and the order was given to restrain the growing numbers of volcano sightseers who were violating the Red Zone boundary.

A section of the north side of the mountain began to swell four and five feet a day as the earth vibrated continuously with harmonics. Molten rock churned beneath the volcano. Ash and steam eruptions alternated with quiet periods. Magma was spewing its way from the center of the earth to the surface below St. Helens, shaking the entire mountain while old Harry gave the news media its daily dosage of "hell" to write about.

The press demanded answers. I waved my hand many times, demanding that whoever was speaking at the time reveal the mountain's intentions. I asked U.S. Forest Service spokesmen. I asked U.S. Geological Survey team scientists. I asked sheriff's deputies. And I asked grocery store operators and Weyerhaeuser maintenance men. And I was not the only eager reporter wanting an answer. Of course, there were no answers.

On Easter Sunday, April 6, U.S. Geological Survey scientist Donal R. Mullineaux speculated that the probability was very low that we in the Northwest might experience a big eruption. None of us English and journalism majors in the press conference audience had any idea what "big" or "imminent" was in geological terms. But we duly reported the facts without too much concern for the context in which they were made.

Two days later, the two craters on top of St. Helens merged during six hours of eruptive fury. The Forest Service and the Geological Survey stood by their pronouncements that a major eruption of molten rock was apparently not imminent. The photos taken for the *Statesman* by Gerry Lewin were suspenseful nonetheless, revealing a hellish gash almost 2,000 feet across and 1,000 feet deep.

The next few weeks were numbing to reporters looking for new angles on the same old story. Scientists waffled between warnings and reassurance. The message that got through to the public was that there was no indication that a major eruption of molten rock would occur in the near future.

Loggers were worried about the powdery ash they found on the snowy slopes near their logging sites. Weyerhaeuser as well as the State of Washington, both dependent on timber harvest revenues, pressed hard for continued operations.

Volcano sightseeing swelled to a regional pastime and T-shirt sales boomed. Ash was bagged and merchandised as though the supply was limited and could run out any time. Plane rides started at $25. Bumper stickers read "Lava or Leave It." Eruptions were certainly dangerous, but the attitude in late April was one of euphoria. Governor Ray expressed Joe Sixpack's sentiments exactly: "I've always said, for many years, that I hoped I lived long enough to see one of our volcanoes erupt."

At last, on April 30, a decision was made. A "Red Zone" closure was imposed around the mountain.

Lee Mattson would have to stew. No way would the deputy let him cross the roadblock and move his family back to their cabin.

Stanley Lee, Dot Elmire, Don Platt and the many other businesspeople lucky enough to be located just outside the Red Zone could remain open, but there were travel restrictions.

Weyerhaeuser could continue logging.

The western edge of the Red Zone skirted the foot of the mountain, about three miles from the summit and 1,000 yards west of the volcano's base. The line defined the boundary between Gifford Pinchot National Forest on the east and Weyerhaeuser's timber on the west.

The northern boundary was two miles beyond the eastern arm of Spirit Lake and roughly 14 miles from the summit.

The eastern boundary was eight miles from the summit while the southernmost point extended about six miles from the summit.

The Red Zone boundary and closure rules allowed Weyerhaeuser to continue logging and did not limit people from major flood threatened areas around and below Swift Reservoir to the south of St. Helens should an eruption occur.

While the Red Zone issue was being debated, sightseers from Maine to Minnesota, towing house trailers and driving big motorhomes, skirted sheriffs' roadblocks to get their vacation views of the ash plumes. Volcano watching, sharing in the collective uncertainty of the region, became a form of outdoor recreation.

The government on the other hand developed a bizarre form of schizophrenia throughout April. Fingerpointing became a regional pastime for responsible officials at every level of government when we in the media put them on the spot with questions about public safety. With the official April 30 Red Zone closure, the government took a firm stand, though it can be argued —and has been—that the limits of the closure were insufficient. Certain Blue Zones were open to loggers during daylight hours and to property owners with special permits. Red Zone violators were subject to $500 fines and six-month jail sentences.

The only exception to the Red Zone edict was Harry Truman. Sheriff Closner was advised by the county prosecutor that Harry could do as he pleased, just as he had always done.

During the April rumblings of St. Helens, *Statesman* reporter Postrel and I worked our way as close in to the Red Zone as possible for what we felt were stirring interviews with the locals. We competed for their opinions with an army of news correspondents who flooded into the area from around the world. This was world news and the major dailies throughout the Seattle

Portland corridor were not about to be outdone by outsiders.

Deputy sheriffs manning roadblocks across Spirit Lake Highway learned the meaning of the word insouciance from *Time* and *Newsweek* magazine photographers assigned to St. Helens while waiting for the next war in the Middle East or Central America. They threatened and bullied their way through roadblocks.

Like grunts in the trenches, the pencil press envied the mobility of the star correspondents from the big Seattle and Portland television stations. Helicopters ferried them over roadblocks. Well dressed from the waist up, the TV folks smoothed their mussed hairdos between "takes" with battery-packed blowdryers. They were pampered because ABC, NBC and CBS were footing the bills for live video feed in case of a big blast.

The story had the local air charter pilots rubbing their palms, too. They bartered hard for reporters' credit cards. They hinted at discounts if a reporter promised a brief mention of their name in the news columns. Thus the big story unfolded.

I for one wanted an interview with some irrascible old coot known as Harry Truman. Saltine wit, a boaster and defiant in the "give-'em-hell" tradition of his namesake, Harry would be an easy front-page story, and that was all I cared about.

My quarry was Page 1 and that did not include 70 years of YMCA campers experiencing the mysteries and miseries of summer camp at Spirit Lake. Youthful campers trooping around the woods, trading blocks of Hershey's chocolate for comic books and committing the suicide of skinnydipping in the ice water of Spirit Lake were not the stuff Mr. Davies was interested in before my deadline, which arrived promptly at 7 p.m., every evening.

My mission assigned by Mr. Davies was to witness a geological event, interpreted by the U.S. Geological Survey. When time permitted, I was to sandwich "people sidebars" between the "straight news" volcano stories of the day.

The ultimate subject, of course, was old Harry, a perfect Page 1 story to lead the paper, illustrated of course with a color photo. We reporters took Harry's fiery comments about a geological phenomenon of which he had no technical understanding and put them in quotations. Harry was a clever fellow, the way he used us in the media. But we were clever, too, the way we used old Harry to help promote our bylines. And not a few editors realized the appeal of those Truman vignettes to sell advertisers on special, souvenir tabloid issues as well.

Explosions that had enlarged two craters atop St. Helens towards the end of March continued to grow through April. Pulverized rock and steam filled the night sky. The old man of St. Helens Lodge, encouraged by us in the media, maintained his vigil over Spirit Lake while others around him evacuated their belongings and cleared out for the time being. We in the media latched onto Truman's defiance out of desperation for something new to report. The death of the old man's favorite cat made the national news wire of The Associated Press.

In May, rain drizzled on my story. Mr. Davies queried me carefully each morning to make sure I had a legitimate subject before he would allow me yet another volcano story. I began yielding to the pressures from the city desk to follow up on assignments unrelated to the volcano story. Readers were bored with the uncertainty of an eruption. This week or this century? Mr. Scarborough was fed up, too, after six weeks of imminent death and destruction stories. Even Harry Truman being knocked out of his bed by an earthquake failed to make Page 1.

The rain let up Saturday, May 17. Cowlitz and Skamania county sheriff's departments braced for the blockade running tourists certain to invade the Red Zone, despite the threats of fines and even jail. Volcano crowd control was becoming routine, just as was everything else about the fuming mountain.

The veil of innocent uncertainty was lifted Sunday morning, May 18, 8:32 a.m. A wide-eyed young man in a navy watchcap, awake and alert at his U.S. Geological Survey post opposite the mountain, keyed his radio microphone hard for a split-second testament before he was blown to bits by the potent force of our world in chaos:

"Vancouver! Vancouver! This is it! . . . Is the transmitter working?"

I was asleep in my northeast Salem house. The phone rang. John H. McMillan, publisher of the Salem, Oregon *Statesman-Journal,* rousted me out of bed to cover what turned out to be the disappearance of 1,300 feet of the summit and the horrible deaths of 57 people. A quarter cubic mile of ash blotted out the light that day for residents living a thousand miles away. Hot volcanic debris devastated 235 square miles that Sunday, killing hundreds of thousands of animals and destroying numerous bridges and homes.

When the smoke cleared and the full impact of the blast settled in, I realized my folly. I had lost something precious. The blast denied me the opportunity to hike, camp, hunt or climb around Mount St. Helens as it had existed. I would not be able to take a cabin at Harmony Falls Lodge or rent a boat from Harry Truman or send my kids to the YMCA camp on the north shore of Spirit Lake.

Years later, I re-created in my mind the peacefulness, the serenity, that Mount St. Helens represented to many thousands of people. I pieced together my own impression of the resiliency of those Spirit Lake people.

139

It took me awhile, but I also came to recognize that the uncertainty of Mount St. Helens, breathing with unpredictable volatility, is the same uncertainty life poses for all of us. But here is some good news: While the rich forestland and many of those Spirit Lake people are gone, smoke and ash cannot and did not snuff out their indomitable human spirit.

Credits for Photographs